AGING
AND ETHNICITY
TOWARD AN
INTERFACE

by

Leo Driedger
University of Manitoba

and

Neena L. Chappell
University of Manitoba

Butterworths
Toronto and Vancouver

Aging and Ethnicity: Toward an Interface
© 1987 Butterworths, A division of Reed Inc.

Printed and bound in Canada

The Butterworth Group of Companies
Canada
Butterworths, Toronto and Vancouver
United Kingdom
Butterworth & Co. (Publishers) Ltd., London and Edinburgh
Australia
Butterworth Pty Ltd., Sydney, Melbourne, Brisbane, Adelaide and Perth
New Zealand
Butterworths (New Zealand) Ltd., Wellington and Auckland
Singapore
Butterworth & Co. (Asia) Pte. Ltd., Singapore
South Africa
Butterworth Publishers (SA) (Pty) Ltd., Durban and Pretoria
United States
Butterworth Legal Publishers, Boston, Seattle, Austin and St. Paul
D&S Publishers, Clearwater

Canadian Cataloguing in Publication Data

Driedger, Leo, 1928-
  Aging and ethnicity

(Perspectives on individual and population aging)
Bibliography: p.
Includes index.
ISBN 0-409-81187-4

1. Minority aged. 2. Minority aged – Social
aspects. 3. Ethnicity. 4. Aging. 5. Aged.
I. Chappell, Neena L. II. Title. III. Series.

HQ1061.D75 1986   305.2'6   C86-094908-7

Sponsoring Editor: Janet Turner
Managing Editor: Linda Kee
Supervisory Editor: Marie Graham
Editor: Anne Butler
Cover Design: Patrick Ng
Production: Jim Shepherd

To our families

BUTTERWORTHS PERSPECTIVES ON INDIVIDUAL AND POPULATION AGING SERIES

The initiation of this Series represents an exciting and significant development for gerontology in Canada. Since the production of Canadian-based knowledge about individual and population aging is expanding rapidly, students, scholars and practitioners are seeking comprehensive yet succinct summaries of the literature on specific topics. Recognizing the common need of this diverse community of gerontologists, Janet Turner, Sponsoring Editor at Butterworths, conceived the idea of a series of specialized monographs that could be used in gerontology courses to complement existing texts and, at the same time, to serve as a valuable reference for those initiating research, developing policies, or providing services to elderly Canadians.

Each monograph includes a state-of-the-art review and analysis of the Canadian-based scientific and professional knowledge on the topic. Where appropriate for comparative purposes, information from other countries is introduced. In addition, some important policy and program implications of the current knowledge base are discussed, and unanswered policy and research questions are raised to stimulate further work in the area. The monographs have been written for a wide audience: undergraduate students in a variety of gerontology courses; graduate students and research personnel who need a summary and analysis of the Canadian literature prior to initiating research projects; practitioners who are involved in the daily planning and delivery of services to aging adults; and policy-makers who require current and reliable information in order to design, implement and evaluate policies and legislation for an aging population.

The decision to publish a monograph on a specific topic has been based in part on the relevance of the topic for the academic and professional community, as well as on the extent of information available at the time an author is signed to a contract. Thus, not all the conceivable topics are included in the early stages of the Series and some topics are published earlier rather than later. Because gerontology in Canada is attracting large numbers of highly qualified graduate students as well as increasingly active research personnel in academic, public and private settings, new areas of concentrated research will evolve. Hence, additional monographs that review and analyze work in these areas will be needed to reflect the evolution of knowledge on specialized topics pertaining to individual or population aging in Canada.

Before introducing the second monograph in the Series, I would like, on behalf of the Series' authors and the gerontology community, to acknowledge the following members of the Butterworths "team" and their respective staffs for their unique and sincere contribution to gerontology in Canada: Geoffrey Burn, President, for his continuing support of the project despite difficult times in the Canadian publishing industry; Janet Turner, Sponsoring Editor, for her vision, endurance and high academic standards; Linda Kee, Managing Editor, for her coordination of the production, especially her constant reminders to authors (and the Series Editor) that the hands of the clock continue to move in spite of our perceptions that manuscript deadlines were still months or years away; Jim Shepherd, Production Manager, for nimbly vaulting many a technical obstacle; and Gloria Vitale, Academic Sales Manager, for her support and promotion of the Series. For each of you, we hope the knowledge provided in this Series will have personal value — but not until well into the next century!

Barry D. McPherson

FOREWORD

The 1981 Census reports that about 17 percent of Canadians are foreign-born. Of this group, 32 percent indicate that their ethnic origin is other than British or French. Moreover, these percentages are even higher for the older age categories. For example, 11 percent of those over 65 years of age in 1981 reported that they spoke a language at home other than French or English. Clearly, the multicultural character of Canada is reflected in our older age groups. This demographic profile has important policy and program implications for those working with older ethnic Canadians, whether in a community or an institutionalized setting.

The first monograph in this Series (McDaniel, S., *Canada's Aging Population*) indicated that shifting immigration policies since the late 1800s have influenced the age and sex distribution, and the geographic location, of Canada's ethnic groups. In this second monograph, two further important findings concerning the relationship between ethnicity and aging are identified and discussed. First, it is noted that the process of aging and the status of the aged varies between ethnic groups because of such factors as: the year(s) they arrived in Canada; the community and province where they settled; their degree of assimilation into the dominant culture; and, the extent to which they have experienced discrimination at different stages in their life-cycle. A second finding is that many Canadian institutions and policies for the elderly have been designed for members of the dominant culture. This practice has occurred because of a failure to recognize that Canada's older population represents a heterogeneous group with different histories, needs and concerns. As a result, policies, programs and services have often failed to adequately meet the needs of older Canadians with diverse cultural, ethnic, language or religious backgrounds.

This monograph critically reviews recent research and policy literature from two complementary perspectives — ethnic studies (Professor Driedger) and social gerontology (Professor Chappell). This unique integration of knowledge from two fields of study is reflected in the creative linkage of assimilation theory (from the ethnic studies field) and modernization theory (from social gerontology). This merger provides an integrated framework whereby the policy implications of aging within an ethnic context can be examined.

Professors Driedger and Chappell begin their monograph by defining ethnicity and aging, and by presenting a demographic profile of when "typical" ethnic groups emigrated to Canada, and where they settled. Specifically, we learn that aging is a more important concern for some ethnic groups than for others, partly because of their history, values, life chances, lifestyles and place of residence. To illustrate the extreme cases, the authors note that 16.5 percent of Canadian Jews are over 65 years of age, and that they primarily live in large urban centres. In contrast, only 3.5 percent of aboriginal Canadians are over 65, and most live in the remote northlands.

In Chapter Two the authors address two basic questions concerning aging ethnic groups in Canada:

- With increased modernization do the elderly lose status and to what extent does this vary by ethnicity?
- Do ethnic groups vary in the extent to which they assimilate or retain their identity, and how do these patterns affect the elderly?

Chapter Three explores the extent to which elements of assimilation and modernization (e.g., education, urbanism, occupational status, use of modern technology, language used at home, religion) affect the lives of Canada's ethnic elderly. Based on this analysis, the authors introduce the concept of "eth-elder", and construct a typology of aging ethnic groups that will enable policy-makers and practitioners to more adequately understand and meet the diverse needs of aging ethnic Canadians. This typology will also stimulate scholars in many fields (e.g., ethnic studies, gerontology, social work, sociology and psychology) to engage in further research and policy analysis about this neglected segment of the elderly population.

In Chapter Four, the role of primary group relations for maintaining ethnic identity and for preventing loss of status within the family is discussed in detail. The concluding chapter presents a revision of the eth-elder typology, a discussion of methodological issues to be considered when studying the ethnic elderly, a research agenda to guide future basic and evaluation research, and a critical review of existing social policies as they pertain to ethnic groups.

In summary, this monograph introduces practitioners, researchers and students to recent and important ideas about aging Canadians with ethnic roots. The discussions of assimilation, modernization, ethnic identity, change of status, and primary group relations will sensitize policy-makers and practitioners to the significance of ethnicity in the aging process, particularly during the later years. The concept of "eth-elder" and the typology of aging ethnic groups will greatly assist gerontologists as they work with aging ethnic Canadians, and will generate further research by scholars in a number of disciplines. Finally, and perhaps most importantly, the monograph provides students in sociology, social work, psychology, recreation, ethnic studies and gerontology (our future practitioners, policy-makers, teachers and researchers) with a comprehensive, current and critical analysis of aging and ethnicity in Canada.

Barry D. McPherson, Ph.D.
Series Editor
Waterloo, Ontario, Canada
November, 1986

PREFACE

This volume represents the collaboration of two sociologists in the two distinct fields of ethnicity and aging. Driedger, who specializes in ethnicity, claims no unique expertise in aging. Chappell, who specializes in aging, can say the same about ethnicity.

When Barry McPherson, the Editor of this Series, asked each of us to contribute to the Series, we discussed it and suggested that we combine our efforts to write a volume on aging and ethnicity. Except for an issue of *Canadian Ethnic Studies*, edited by Victor Ujimoto, very little work had been done in Canada combining the two fields of study. When we examined literature that combined the two fields in the United States and elsewhere, including a volume by Donald Gelfand, *Aging: The Ethnic Factor*, we found that much still remained to be done.

Here we present to you *Aging and Ethnicity: Toward an Interface*. This is our attempt at integrating the two fields. The challenge was to find conceptual models that would provide a framework for comparison in aging and ethnicity. We have used the theories of modernization in aging and assimilation in ethnicity for that task. Our special readers and critics think that a combination of the two work well; we hope the reader will think so too. Another challenge was to provide a conceptual context for those who are more theoretically inclined, as well as present more practical information for practitioners who deal with everyday policy and action. A third challenge was to do all this when models and theories were still limited, and when data were often not available. All of these problems were a challenge, and we hope the reader will find this volume useful, even though in some ways it may be a bit premature.

In addition to the many listed in the references whose writings stimulated us, we wish to thank Barry McPherson, Editor of this Series, and Janet Turner of Butterworths for their encouragement and suggestions. We also wish to thank reviewers Carolyn Rosenthal and Margaret Penning who provided critical comments that helped improve the manuscript. Marilyn Shantz patiently typed many versions of the manuscript, and Audrey Blandford ran much data on the computer, for which we thank them.

Leo Driedger and Neena Chappell
University of Manitoba
1986

CONTENTS

Butterworths Perspectives on Individual and Population Aging Series   v
Foreword vii
Preface ix
List of Tables xiii
List of Figures xv

Chapter 1: Introduction 1

Definitions of Ethnicity and Aging 2
   The Ethnic Factor 4
   Perspectives on Aging and Ethnicity 4
   Problems of Eth-elderly Status 5
   Policy Implications 6
A Demographic Overview 7
   The Foreign-born Elderly 9
   Gender Differentials 11
Summary 11

Chapter 2: Perspectives on Aging and Ethnicity 13

Theories of Aging 14
   Age Stratification 15
Cowgill's Modernization Model 19
   Health Technology 20
   Economic Technology 21
   Urbanization 21
   Education 22
   Criticisms 23
   Modifications 25
   Modernization and Ethnicity 26
Park's Assimilation Theory 27
   Multicultural Pluralism: The Ethnic Mosaic 28
   Modifications of the Ideal Polarities 29
Toward a Theoretical Interface between Aging and Ethnicity ... 32
Summary 34

Chapter 3: The Ethnic Factor 35

Ethnic Elderly and Social Change 35
   Education as a Form of Modernization 35

Urbanism as Modernization 36
Occupational Status and Modern Technology 37
Assimilation and Home Language Use 40
Religion as a Support for Ethnic Elderly 42
Finding Eth-elder Types 46
Regional Variation 46
Traditional Aboriginal Elderly 48
Urban Jewish Elderly 53
European Prairie Farm Elders 55
Elderly of the French Charter Minority 56
Myth of the British Majority Type 58
Summary 60

Chapter 4:   Social Status and Eth-elder Roles 63

Support for Eth-elders 65
American Ethnic Elderly and Support Patterns 67
Informal Networks of Canadian Ethnic Elders 69
Supportiveness of Ethnic Group Membership 73
Formal Services: An Ethnic Disadvantage? 75
Some Canadian Evidence 78
Cumulative Disadvantages 80
Summary 83

Chapter 5:   Policy Considerations 87

Eth-elder Needs and Social Policy 87
Age Versus Need 87
Meeting the Needs of Eth-elders 88
The Importance of Community 92
Returning to Ethnic Types 94
Urban High Status Type 94
Rural Low Status Type 96
Rural High Status Type 97
Urban Low Status Type 98
Visible Minorities 99
French Charter Type 99
British Charter Type 100
Basic Principles 101
Research Requirements 102
Evaluation Research and Needs Assessments 105
Conclusions 107

Bibliography 109

Index 125

TABLES

1.1   Elderly and Non-elderly Populations by Ethnicity, Canada, 1981 8

1.2   Elderly and Non-elderly Foreign-born Populations by Place of Birth, Canada, 1981 9

2.1   The Aged: Arguments For and Against Minority Status 17

3.1   Education Level of Canada's Elderly (55 Years and Over) by Ethnic Groups 36

3.2   Percentage of Ethnic Elderly (55 Years and Older) in Ten Metropolitan Centres of Canada, 1981 38

3.3   Occupational Status of Ethnic Groups in Canada (Aged 55 and Over) in 1981 39

3.4   Mother Tongue by Ethnic Groups and Their Home Language Use, Aged 65 and Over in Canada, 1981 41

3.5   Percentage of Ethnic Group Shifting to English Mother Tongue, by Age Group, Canada, 1971 43

3.6   Affiliation of Ethnic Elderly (Age 65 and Over) with Religious Denominations 44

3.7   Distribution of Ethnic Elderly (55 Years Plus) by Province, Canada, 1981 47

3.8   Attitudes and Activity of Native Indian Elderly (50 Years and Older) in Winnipeg, 1984 52

4.1a Ethnicity by Marital Status, Aged 65 and Over, Canada, 1981 .. 70

4.1b Living Arrangement by Ethnicity, Aged 65 and Over, Canada, 1981 71

4.2   Number of Children Ever Born by Ethnicity, Aged 65 and Over, Canada, 1981 73

4.3   Ethnicity by Type of Residence, Manitoba, 1977 80

5.1   Preference for Culturally Relevant Services, Indians Aged 50 and Over, Winnipeg, 1984 90

FIGURES

1.1 Foreign-born and Canadian-born Elderly by Ethnic Origin
in Canada, 1981 10
2.1 Aging and Modernization 20
2.2 Modernization and Assimilation Processes and Goals 33
3.1 Cultural and Linguistic Regions, Canada, 1981 49
3.2 Emerging Eth-elder Types Plotted on a
Traditional-Modern Continuum 61
5.1 Eth-elder Types by Socioeconomic Status and Degree
of Urbanization 95

CHAPTER 1

INTRODUCTION

More than any other age group, the elderly provide the nation with a distinct depository of its multicultural history and life. In folk societies, there are relatively few elderly, but many believe the elderly in such societies are valued for their consciousness of tradition and values, which are transmitted to succeeding generations through oral means. Older persons are also unique in a modern plural society because of their range of historical experiences that bridge the generations. For example, the lives of many aged aboriginal Indians span the enormous shift from a hunting and fishing food-gathering existence to one influenced by the introduction of modern communication and transportation. Unfortunately, moderns are sometimes preoccupied with technical advances and take too little time to learn from these cross-cultural and cross-generational experiences.

Many aboriginal Indians have entered cities without the buffer experience of farming and food production. While few elderly native Indians remain who can tell of their own introduction to reserves, many Indians can remember clearly the stories told by their parents about such traumatic changes. Most treaty elderly know well the Indian reserve and its problems, as well as the considerable movement of males, especially to the mines and cities to work.

On the other hand, most Jewish elders remember well the holocaust of the 1940s. A few lived through it themselves, and almost all can tell stories of the many loved ones of their family who were lost in the ovens of Dachau and Auschwitz. Although many can no longer relate their own experiences in the rural Shtetls of Eastern Europe such as Russia and Poland, accounts told by their parents during long wintery nights in Canada almost make it seem as though they had been there themselves. The trek from the Shtetls to the cities they moved to was a long one, with many pioneering hardships and adjustments.

Most Japanese elderly in Canada today took part in the inland deportation from the west coast during World War II, when they lost most of their property and suffered dislocation and discrimination (Zich 1986). Elderly bachelors in the Chinatowns of inner cities like Vancouver and Toronto watch recent Chinese families enter Canada, a privilege they missed because early Canadian laws did not permit bringing Chinese family members. Many Ukrainian aged left the steppes of Russia, having lived through the

1

revolution and its aftermath, for the aspen belt of the Canadian prairies. These diverse multicultural experiences of Canada's aged represent a patchwork of many kinds. The experiences and needs of the aged today are varied and diverse. Linguistic, cultural, religious, political, and economic variations must be explored and researched.

The elderly today also represent the last survivors of the massive European migrations in the early 1900s when up to 400,000 immigrants arrived in a single year. These immigrants entered the prairies, the west and the Northlands to establish pioneer settlements in the wild. Never again will such a large number of immigrants enter Canada; they are a historical resource that will soon disappear. If oral and written histories of their experiences are not prepared, this historical and cultural resource will be lost forever.

This book on ethnicity and aging is organized around a fourfold task: (1) exploring some of the conceptual and theoretical perspectives that have emerged in both the aging and ethnic literature; (2) examining in some depth the ethnic factor and its importance for the study of the elderly; (3) examining the extent to which aging results in loss of status, and the alternatives, including ethnic identity, that might be available; and (4) assessing what implications aging of the ethnic elderly has for social policy. Many of these issues have not yet been highly researched, and a short volume such as this does not allow dealing with some of these issues in a thorough manner. Nevertheless, the need for studying the ethnic elderly is important — indeed pressing. The interface of aging and ethnicity must begin.

DEFINITIONS OF ETHNICITY AND AGING

Shibutani and Kwan (1965, 47) use the definition of *ethnicity* that Hughes and Hughes (1952, 115) proposed: "An ethnic group consists of those who perceive themselves as being alike by virtue of their common ancestry, real or factitious, and who are so regarded by others." A sense of belonging to a group, and the collective will to exist are also essential elements of Gordon's (1964, 23–24) thinking, which grows out of the Greek word *ethnos*, meaning "people" or "nation." Early humans often see themselves as "a people" and have a sense of peoplehood including a common culture, beliefs and values within a defined space. Reisman's (1950) "tradition-directed person" usually emerges out of Redfield's (1947, 293–308) "folk society," part of the "ethnos" and the "peoplehood" way of thinking. In sociological theory it is assumed that all humans including British, French, German, Jews, Hutterites, Indians, and all others must belong to an "ethnos." Scholars have the task, then, of sorting out the various foci of ethnic identification (culture, religion, nation, language, etc.), the salience of such identification, and the various shifts that may occur from one form of ethnicity and nationalism to another.

In countries such as Canada and the United States, where most have come as immigrants in the last few centuries, there is the additional task of sorting out which ethnic groups are numerically large (majority or plurality) and which are relatively small (often referred to as ethnic minorities). In addition to size, relative racial, economic, and political power becomes at least as important as numbers. In both Canada and the United States no ethnic group is in the numerical majority, although the British are usually the most numerous, and often also the most powerful. Racially, Caucasians are a very large, dominant majority, while linguistically English is spoken most often. This, however, frequently varies by region.

Aging is the process of development through time and as such refers to the life course or significant portions of it. Old age is usually defined as starting at age 65, but this is a social definition resulting mainly from the establishment of retirement norms and legislation related to old age security payments. It is convenient to use a designated chronological age when speaking of the elderly, as long as it is recognized that it is an approximation. Old age is whenever our health and functioning deteriorates to a level that results in decreasing independence and mobility.

In recognition of the fact that the abilities, needs, and other characteristics of those aged 65 and older vary considerably, it is becoming increasingly common to distinguish three groups (Schreiber 1972; Chappell and Havens 1980): the young old (frequently defined as those age 65 to 74); the middle old (frequently defined as those age 75 to 84) and the old old (frequently defined as those age 85 and over). Even these groupings frequently mask important differences among the elderly. One such difference is variation by ethnicity.

Although some people in all societies seem to have lived as long as people do today, very few reached age 65 in food-gathering societies. This segment of the population is growing worldwide today. While decreases in infant mortality and concomitant increases in the proportions of elderly began in the economically advanced nations of Europe and European settlements (Hauser 1976), rapid cultural diffusion of ways of reducing the major causes of mortality spread in the developing countries. This resulted in reduced infant and child mortality without the economic and social development that initially allowed the rising standards of living and declines in mortality among Europeans. The lower birth rate in the developed nations means they have a faster aging population than less developed countries have, while the lower death rate in the developed nations means greater extension of life. This is changing, and it is estimated that by the century's end the less developed countries will have a greater proportion of the world's elderly population (Siegel 1981).

At present, 9.5 percent (2.4 million) of Canada's population is aged 65 and over, a percentage already exceeded in some countries such as England and Wales. The percentage in Canada will peak at around 20 percent when the baby boom generation reaches age 65, around the year 2030. In 1981, the elderly among our Jewish population represented 16.5 percent, and among our aboriginal population represented 3.5 percent, evidence that these proportions vary considerably by ethnic group.

The Ethnic Factor

While the importance of studying ethnic variations among the elderly is gradually being recognized, the dearth of relevant data is striking. Explorations into the meaning of ethnicity, that is, the experience of ethnicity, among the elderly are lacking (Disman 1984). Thus, this book relies rather extensively on the Canadian census, still one of the best sources of longitudinal data for both age and ethnic groups, despite the problems of using such data to study ethnicity (see for example Ryder 1955). The census data permit a sketch to be drawn of the demographic history of immigration, ethnic identification, gender, and the degree to which our population is foreign or native born. It soon becomes apparent that the combinations of ethnic elderly vary enormously by regions. The aboriginal elderly who dominate in the Northlands of Canada are but a tiny (3.5 percent) proportion of the aboriginal population and are primarily located in isolated, rural, often food-gathering areas. The elderly in Newfoundland are almost all of British origin, in Quebec of French origin, and on the prairies of many origins. The Jewish elderly almost all reside in metropolitan cities. This diversity makes our research task both stimulating and complex.

Further, a great deal of change is occurring. Canada's older population is less educated, has less income, and has occupied lower status occupations than younger cohorts. Culturally, home language use and interest in religion is declining, suggesting a reverse trend, with the elderly more ethnically identified with these values. These changes in various directions add to the complexity of understanding Canada's ethnic elderly.

It is not possible to deal with the scores of ethnic origins and trends for each group. Therefore, ethnic types, including traditional aboriginal elderly, metropolitan Jewish elderly, and others, have been devised. Because of their position in society, the Jewish elderly are probably much more able to meet their own needs, while the aboriginals will find it more difficult. These diversified eth-elder types should assist in planning future services. Although the demographic census data are too general for testing more specific trends, they do provide enough comparative information that definite types of eth-elders can be found in various regions of Canada.

Perspectives on Aging and Ethnicity

Conceptually, the field of aging is in its formative beginnings. It is a relatively new field of study. While research is escalating, the difficult work of creating a theoretical base is still very much in the beginning stages. Early attempts wrestled with the problem of disengagement upon retirement, especially in urban areas, but many are looking for a more sophisticated conceptual framework. More general sociological approaches such as exchange theory have also been used, arguing the loss of an exchange base for the retired, leaving them with mostly the resource of compliance. More powerful theories are needed in order to understand aging among ethnic members.

Modernization theory is one of the more comprehensive conceptual developments. Cowgill (1974) suggests that urbanization, education, health, and economic technology converge into a modernization trend that ultimately leads to a loss of social status for the elderly. In Chapter 2 this perspective is enlarged upon and trends are probed to see if indeed modernization leads to loss of status.

There are, however, others who think that the price of modernization is not so great, and to some extent it should and can be resisted, and on occasion redirected. Economic status may not be the only or the major determinant of life satisfaction, prestige, or quality of life, especially for the ethnic elderly. More research is needed to explore the alternatives and explanatory power of theories that are beginning to emerge in the field of aging.

While theoretical developments in ethnicity also need much work, several theories have had their impact for a considerable time. The theory of assimilation of minorities into the larger majority society was well formulated by Park more than 50 years ago (see Hughes 1950). Along with the deterministic interpretations of evolution, it was long assumed that most minorities would not be able to resist the influences of the majority. This theory and others that are beginning to be modified are explored in Chapter 2.

In Canada especially, continued immigration from the Third World is increasingly resulting in more plurality, in linguistic, cultural, religious, and racial arenas. The Bilingual and Bicultural Commission of the 1960s already recognized the increased presence of "other" ethnic groups, resulting in a special volume that stressed multiculturalism (Royal Commission on Bilingualism and Biculturalism 1970). Soon thereafter, Prime Minister Trudeau declared Canada a bilingual and multicultural nation.

There are many parallels between assimilation theory in ethnicity and modernization theory in aging. As scholars have been modifying and revising assimilation theory in ethnicity, scholars have been doing the same with modernization theory in aging. Chapter 3 continues to explore theoretical underpinnings through an examination of existing empirical data as they relate to ethnicity and aging.

Problems of Eth-elderly Status

Proponents of both assimilation and modernization theories assume loss of status as a central focus. Modernizationists assume that with occupational retirement, income will drop and, compared to younger Canadians, the elderly will also fall behind in educational preparedness. With the advance of new technology and urbanization, the elderly lose social status perhaps even before retirement. Assimilationists assume that unless immigrants coming into Canada shed some of their ethnic distinctiveness, they will not be able to compete in the larger society and will not be able to attain the status of native-born Canadians. Status can be achieved through assimilation into the larger whole. Families that emphasize ethnic identity are assumed to be traditional, not modern. In Chapter 4 the relevance of status and assimilation are examined in terms of primary group relations, specifically in light of care and assistance provided to older members of ethnic groups. The issue of alternative statuses is also discussed here.

Are there alternatives other than maintenance of social status through economic prestige? Whereas it is true that such social status is important during the working years, is it still as central after retirement? Is there an alternative to competition for economic status and prestige? Can the elderly also "retire" from this rat race? Some of the research on life satisfaction suggests that occupational prestige and status may be largely a middle class phenomenon, whereas blue collar workers often yearn for release from tedious, unfulfilling work, which technology, bureaucratization, and urbanization often bring with them. Family and friends may be more important than modernization theory assumes.

Policy Implications

Finally, in Chapter 5 policy implications are discussed. A review of the literature shows that much more research needs to be done. There are enormous gaps in the literature; the data base needed for policy making is quite limited and often non-existent. The research methods used in some of the studies leave much to be desired, so that the quality of research also needs to be upgraded. Some of the most pressing research needs are noted.

With the development of eth-elder types, the variety of needs of the ethnic elderly becomes clear, as does the importance of taking the various eth-elderly types into account when designing informal and formal services. For example, Jewish urbanites living in the major cities of Canada are relatively accessible for planning purposes, they are often clustered in large numbers, and they usually possess many of their own financial, educational, and religious resources. The small number of aboriginal elderly, on the other hand, scattered in the Northlands in a food-gathering environment, with limited incomes and education, require vastly different services to satisfy their needs. They are also not easily accessible.

To what extent can various eth-elder types satisfy their own needs; to what extent can their respective ethnic families and communities provide for their needs; and where should municipal, provincial, and federal governments become involved? Answers to such policy questions are hard to find in the literature, and the research to answer such questions is limited.

Before writing this text, we were aware that research on the ethnic elderly was limited, but we were still surprised by the number of gaps that exist and by how much still remains to be done. In this volume, existing literature is reviewed and numerous points at which research on aging and ethnicity can interface or need to interface are suggested. Often the discussion is presented in the form of hypotheses because solid data are lacking. We hope that the text will generate much more research and stimulate data collection.

A DEMOGRAPHIC OVERVIEW

Before turning to a discussion of some of the theoretical perspectives, a macro-demographic overview of aging and ethnicity in Canada provides a needed context for later discussions. Socioeconomic status will be discussed in Chapters 2 and 3. A more detailed exploration of different ethnic types and of the social contexts in which the elderly find themselves in different parts of Canada comes later.

In 1981, there were 2,360,000 Canadians who were aged 65 and over who represented 9.1 percent of the total population of 24 million. The Canadian population is aging considerably, and the proportion of elderly persons is growing. During the past decade (1971–1981) the aged increased by 35 percent, compared with a 13 percent increase for the total population (Statistics Canada 1984).

In 1981 the two charter groups represented two-thirds of the total population of Canada (British 40.2 percent and French 26.7 percent). The aboriginal native Indians represented 1.7 percent; all others made up 23.8 percent; and 7.6 percent were of multiple and mixed origins. No one ethnic group represents a majority, and the people of Canada come from many national, cultural, linguistic, and racial origins. We are a diverse, pluralist nation. Are there demographic variations of the elderly among these many different groups?

Table 1.1 shows that some ethnic groups are aging much more than others. Comparing the two charter groups, it is evident that while 9.1 percent of the Canadian population are 65 years of age or more, a larger proportion of British (11.1 percent) and a smaller portion of French (7.8 percent) are more than 65. Among the other groups, the Jews (16.5 percent), Poles (14.5 percent), and Ukrainians (13.7 percent) are older than the average, while the native peoples (3.5 percent) are very much younger.

The differences between Jewish and native elderly are enormous. The 16.5 percent of the Jews who are over 65 represent a very large proportion of that group, as large as the European countries with the highest proportion of elderly today. They also represent the approximate proportion who

TABLE 1.1

ELDERLY AND NON-ELDERLY POPULATIONS BY ETHNICITY, CANADA, 1981

Ethnicity	Per 100 of Age Group		Per 100 of Total	
	0–64	65+	0–64	65+
British	39.3	49.3	88.9	11.1
French	27.1	23.0	92.2	7.8
British/French*	1.9	0.8	96.0	4.0
Jewish	1.0	2.0	83.5	16.5
Polish	1.0	1.7	85.5	14.5
Ukrainian	2.1	3.3	86.3	13.7
German	4.7	5.4	89.7	10.3
Dutch	1.7	1.4	92.5	7.5
Chinese	1.2	0.9	93.3	6.7
Italian	3.2	2.3	93.3	6.7
All other	14.7	9.2	94.1	5.9
Native peoples	2.2	0.8	96.5	3.5
Totals	100.0	100.0	90.9	9.1

* Multiple response.

NOTE: This table includes British, French and British/French, plus the eight ethnic origins (single response) with the largest counts for the total population. These latter ethnic origins are arranged here by descending proportions of the aged population (last column).

SOURCE: Statistics Canada, *The Elderly in Canada*, Table 8, p. 16 (Ottawa: Minister of Supply and Services, 1984). Reproduced with permission.

will be elderly in all of Canada at the turn of the century. Very few older persons exist among the aboriginals (3.5 percent). Canada as a whole had more than this proportion at the time of Confederation (4.5 percent). These demographic differences will have important implications for any policies that might be needed in relating in these groups of aging people. In a sense, the Jews and native peoples can be thought of as opposite polar types with very different demographic profiles. They can be enlarged upon later as prototypes.

The Italians and Chinese, like the native peoples, have smaller proportions of elderly, while the Poles and Ukrainians are more like the Jews. The two charter groups tend to gravitate toward the average, with the British leaning toward the Jewish and the French toward the native proportions. What this means is that the needs of the many Jewish elderly are basically different from those of their relatively few native counterparts. In the rest of this chapter some of the variables that affect aging are isolated, to provide a better understanding of what the different needs and resources might be.

Approaches and policies will have to vary to meet the needs of the different types.

The Foreign-born Elderly

In 1981 about one-sixth (16.9 percent) of the Canadian population were foreign-born (Table 1.2). These first-generation Canadians come from many parts of the world and usually speak their mother tongue and practise their ethnic culture more than do members of later generations. The proportion of foreign-born in Canada has been declining steadily. Earlier, the foreign-born proportions were much larger because of the very large migrations that occurred. Some of these larger proportions of foreign-born probably still reflect different ethnic needs among the elderly. There is some evidence that a few who come to Canada later return to their home country when they retire, but this seems to be only a trickle.

While the British (35 percent) represent more than one-third of all foreign-born elderly (aged 65 plus), almost no French elderly (.6 percent) are foreign-born (see Table 1.2 and Figure 1.1). This is due to continued British immigration to Canada in large numbers; French immigration has been very minimal. The French, of course, have been in Canada the longest of all

TABLE 1.2

ELDERLY AND NON-ELDERLY FOREIGN-BORN POPULATIONS BY PLACE OF BIRTH, CANADA, 1981

Place of Birth	Per 100 of Age Group		Per 100 of Total	
	0–64	65+	0–64	65+
United Kingdom	20.4	35.0	74.2	25.8
France	1.6	0.6	93.0	7.0
U.S.S.R.	2.1	9.4	52.2	47.8
Poland	3.0	8.0	64.9	35.1
United States of America	7.4	11.4	76.2	23.8
Netherlands	3.8	2.4	88.7	11.3
Italy	10.7	6.4	89.3	10.7
Germany	5.5	3.2	89.4	10.6
All other	41.2	22.7	90.0	10.0
Portugal	4.2	0.9	95.7	4.3
Totals	100.0	100.0	83.1	16.9

NOTE: This table includes the United Kingdom and France, plus the seven countries of birth with the largest counts for the total population. These latter countries are arranged here by descending proportions of the aged population (last column).

SOURCE: Statistics Canada, *The Elderly in Canada*, Table 7, p. 16 (Ottawa: Minister of Supply and Services, 1984). Reproduced with permission.

FIGURE 1.1

FOREIGN-BORN AND CANADIAN-BORN ELDERLY
BY ETHNIC ORIGIN IN CANADA, 1981

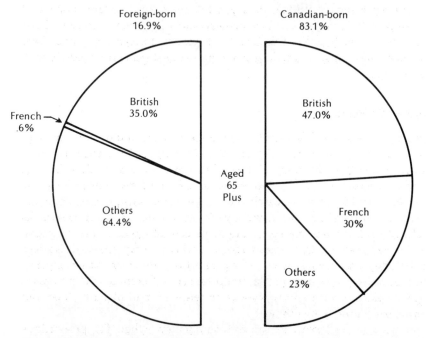

SOURCE: Statistics Canada, *The Elderly in Canada*, Table 7, p. 16 (Ottawa: Minister of Supply and Services, 1984). Reproduced with permission.

European settlers, and in this respect they are fairly unique. Other elderly (except for the native peoples) make up two-thirds of the foreign-born population (64.4 percent).

The proportion of elderly among the foreign-born also varies considerably by ethnic group. Almost one-half (47.8 percent) of the foreign-born Russians are elderly compared to very few of the Portuguese (4.3 percent) (Statistics Canada 1981). This again illustrates the varied history of migration of each ethnic group. Large proportions of Russian, Polish, and British immigrants arrived in Canada earlier than other immigrants, and significant numbers of these have now reached the age of 65 or more. On the other hand, most Portuguese immigrants arrived later, and very few of their numbers have yet become elderly (4.3 percent).

However, the ethnic proportions of Canadian-born elders looks very different. The British represent almost one-half (47 percent) of all the Canadian-born elderly, the French almost one-third (30 percent), and all others less than one-fourth (23 percent). Foreign-born elders are very heavily skewed toward non-charter Canadians, while Canadian-born elders more closely represent the total Canadian population.

These statistics on the foreign-born are very important in the study of needs for the aged. The foreign-born factor is of no significance when dealing with the French-Canadian elderly, while the needs of a large portion of foreign-born British elderly (25.8 percent) must be taken seriously. Other ethnic elderly such as the Russians (47.8 percent foreign-born) and Poles (35.1 percent) represent even larger numbers of first-generation elderly with special needs.

Gender Differentials

The proportions of women and men who are 65 years and older varies over time and by marital status. Before 1951 the number of elderly men was always greater than the number of elderly women. However, after 1951 the sex ratio reversed, so that by 1981 there were four elderly women for every three men. In 1981 women over 85 outnumbered men two to one. The marital status of elderly men and women varies even more. While three-fourths of all elderly men were married, only 40 percent of women were. One-half (49 percent) of the women were widowed, whereas only one-sixth (14 percent) of the men were widowers. The proportions who were either single or divorced did not vary by sex. This important sex differential, either in terms of proportions of men and women or in terms of marital status, does not seem to vary greatly be ethnicity.

Immigration does affect the sex differentials somewhat. The proportions of French males and females are identical (remember there was little immigration of the French); there are somewhat more British females than males; and more male others (non-charter immigrants) than females (these groups have arrived in larger numbers more recently). In Canada's early past, more immigrant males, especially single males, than females came to find work. Chinese males (both maried and unmarried) were imported to help build the CPR railroad in the 1880s, and later severe legal restrictions made it impossible for their families to join them if they were married. Thus, many of the elderly Chinese in cities like Vancouver and Toronto are bachelors.

SUMMARY

We have presented some basic descriptive demographic information on ethnic variation within the elderly population in Canada. The demographic eth-elder variation and heterogeneity in Canada is striking. Immigration, gender, and marital status all add to the mosaic. Regional eth-elder clustering, to be examined later, adds to the complexity of ethnic and aging research. This demographic survey has been presented to provide a context for the remainder of the book. It also points to distinguishable eth-elder types for policy considerations to be discussed later.

CHAPTER 2

PERSPECTIVES ON AGING AND ETHNICITY

The potential importance of ethnicity for aging has generally been accepted by gerontological scholars. Researchers have, however, turned more attention to this area in the United States than in Canada. American scholars have tended to focus on blacks and chicanos, groups not particularly appropriate for the study of the elderly in Canada. Further, they have tended to study minority groups rather than ethnicity per se. In the area of ethnicity, age in general has been used as a control variable, but there is almost no focus on aging as such. The linkage between these two areas has hardly begun.

To add to the problem of integration, each field has had fairly distinct foci. Major concerns in ethnic studies frequently centre around questions of ethnic identity (both voluntary and involuntary) and the effect of ethnic identity on status and mobility. Issues involving stereotypes, prejudices, and discrimination against visible minorities (non-caucasians) has consequently received much attention. Voluntarily retaining a separate identity (as found, for example, among the Hutterites, Jews, Indians, and French-Canadians), and the consequences of such retention on mobility, have also received considerable attention. Thus, freedom, justice, and equality have all been important factors in studying mobility aspirations.

In gerontology, there has been a major emphasis on individual adjustment to aging, both to the inevitable deterioration in health that accompanies aging and to the exit from major social roles, primarily paid labour and child rearing. Studies on adjustment have tended to concentrate on concepts such as life satisfaction, morale, and subjective well-being. Indeed, Jansen and Mueller (1983) estimate from a casual survey of the literature that around 30 percent of journal space in social gerontology addresses correlates of well-being among the old. A related concern surrounds the maintenance of an acceptable quality of life, which includes a satisfactory level of self-sufficiency. A considerable amount of work also relates to the question of status, usually the status of the elderly compared with those who are not elderly.

Despite their differences, both the area of ethnicity and of aging have a concern with social status and therefore with justice and equality. A discussion of two theories, one prominent in each area, clarifies this commonality and permits a focused examination of a number of issues where aging and ethnicity can interface. In this chapter we discuss modernization theory from the field of aging and assimilation theory from the field of ethnicity, to provide common ground in areas that frequently explore very different questions.

THEORIES OF AGING

As a multidisciplinary, substantive area, gerontology has tended to borrow theoretical frameworks from established disciplines and apply them to concerns at hand rather than elaborate theory development particular to its own area. In addition, gerontology is relatively new, which means theory development has not had time to mature.

One of the first attempts at theory building in social gerontology (we are not interested here in biological or physiological theories of aging) is represented by the disengagement theory of aging. It was first described by Cumming and associates in 1960 and subsequently elaborated in 1961 and 1964. Disengagement theory arose as a response to the activity theory of aging, which claims that people seek activity and involvement in social life as they age (Havighurst and Albrecht 1953). Activity theory argues that optimum aging means maintaining activity levels in old age that are similar to those in middle age. Decreases that do occur are due to societal withdrawal from the elderly. In other words, high social involvement and activity are key components of successful aging.

In contrast, disengagement theorists claim there is a mutual withdrawal by both society and the elderly themselves. Decreased emotional investment in persons and objects in the environment and decreased interaction with others is accompanied by an increased preoccupation with the self. Proponents suggest that disengagement begins during middle life, involving a sense of shortness of time and evaluations of what has been done, with a shift away from achievement. The aged may feel doubt about the value of their achievements, and losses may outrun ability to replace them. Crucial in the disengagement process is finding a new set of rewards. Freedom from obligations replaces the constraint of being needed; the disengaged person is free. Some say the ability to enjoy old age is the ability and the opportunity to use freedom (Cumming and Henry 1961, 25). There will be a tendency not to replace broken ties, and once withdrawal has begun, it may become more difficult to make new contacts. There is also disengagement from previous roles. Roles related to work, to children, and for some, a spouse, all change as work, children, and spouses become independent or die. There is also a dearth of role models for retired people.

The theory has received heavy criticism because it postulates the process of disengagement as universal, mutual and desirable, and inevitable. As A. M. Rose (1968) summarizes, critics of inevitability maintain that those who are non-engaged in the later years are those who have a life-long pattern of non-engagement that is continued into old age, while critics of desirability claim that disengagement may occur, but it is not desirable and leads to lessened satisfaction. Maddox (1968) and Havighurst et al. (1968) report empirical data showing that more involvement and activity is associated with greater life satisfaction. Further, the theory was developed from studying a sample of elderly who were in good health and independent financially.

Although much effort was spent in the 1960s and part of the 1970s debating whether the disengagement or activity theory best explained adjustment during old age, neither stood the test of time. Theories used in gerontology since that time have tended to be borrowed or adapted from the disciplines of their authors. Several are evident in the literature, including the aged as a subculture, elaborated primarily by A. M. Rose (1968); labelling theory (Kuypers and Bengtson 1973); modernization theory (Cowgill and Holmes 1972); the aged as a minority (Barron 1953); aging as exchange (Dowd 1980); age stratification theory (Riley 1971); and the double and multiple jeopardy, or conversely age-as-leveller, hypotheses (Dowd and Bengtson 1978). These are not always distinct from one another. Modernization and aging as exchange are related. Both the aged as a minority and the jeopardy hypotheses derive from age stratification theory.

Interest here lies primarily in exploring modernization theory in order to compare it with assimilation theory in ethnicity. Before doing that, however, the aged as a minority and the jeopardy hypotheses are examined briefly. They represent attempts to link aging directly with ethnicity, and both have received attention in the literature.

Age Stratification

Age stratification theorists note that societies tend to be ordered into hierarchies of age strata, with appropriate norms and obligations associated with each stratum (Riley 1971; Riley et al. 1972). Social roles are patterned and distributed to and within age strata. A process of allocation involves the assigning and reassigning of people of various ages into suitable roles. A process of socialization ensures a smooth transition of individuals from one age status to the next. Because each age group experiences a unique history, and because the social and psychological characteristics of each group may vary, the patterns of aging differ from one generation to the next as they pass through and live within each age stratum.

Two perspectives that derive from age stratification theory are the minority group and double and multiple jeopardy hypotheses. Debate on whether or not it is appropriate to characterize the elderly as a minority group is longstanding. A minority can be defined, following Wirth (1945), as a group of people who are accorded differential and unequal treatment because of physical or cultural characteristics. The group may regard itself as an object of collective discrimination. The debate about whether the elderly are a minority depends on whether all elderly can be compared to racial or ethnic minorities. Some do try to apply the minority concept to a subgroup (rather than all) of the aged.

In the 1950s and 1960s Barron (1953; 1954; 1961) argued that the aged are an emerging quasi-minority group, that their economic, psychological, and social situation in urban, industrial America resembles that of the many ethnic groups that are minorities. The aged are subjected to stereotyping, prejudice, and discrimination at the attitudinal and behavioural levels, they react with self-consciousness, sensitivity, self-hatred, and defensiveness, and legislation against discrimination has been enacted. The aged, however, are also found in all families, whether of majority or minority status, high or low social status. They therefore cannot be unique subgroups functioning independently, that is, they cannot be true minorities.

Palmore (1969) also argued that the aged exhibit four major minority-group characteristics: others have negative stereotypes about the aged, the aged are segregated both voluntarily and involuntarily, they are discriminated against, and like minorities they react in a similar way to prejudice and discrimination. However, the elderly were not born into their age group and do not as yet have strong group identity or political unity (Palmore and Manton 1973).

Discussing primarily the aged in Canada, Jarvis (1972) states that old people are a minority group because they are clearly visible as a distinct category, they are discriminated against, they have come to define themselves as inferior, and increasingly they are forming pressure groups to exert political power. Newman (1973) also considers the aged a minority group, based primarily on their physical distinctions and subordinate power position.

In their summary and assessment of the literature on the aged as a minority group, Abu-Laban and Abu-Laban (1980) reveal the lack of agreement on the criteria used (see Table 2.1) and the conclusions reached. For example, some use the visibility of the aged as an aspect of minority status, others do not. While most agree with a general pattern of disadvantage, not all accept it as sufficient for minority-group status. Some argue for the subordinate social position of the elderly, others point to their overrepresentation in positions of political power. Abu-Laban and Abu-Laban conclude that the experiential component of subordination shared by the elderly with racial and ethnic minorities has been well articulated. Less attention has been given to the structural component. It is the structural element, they argue, that is not shared with traditional minorities, because the elderly are part of both majority and minority families. They point out further that

TABLE 2.1

THE AGED: ARGUMENTS FOR AND AGAINST MINORITY STATUS

For	Against
Physical Characteristics 1. Visibility (Atchley 1972; Breen 1960; Jarvis 1972; Newman 1973)	1. Not constant through life cycle (Streib 1965) 2. No agreement on parameters of agedness (Streib)
Sociocultural Characteristics 1. Subordinate social status (Atchley; Barron 1953; Gubrium 1973; Jarvis; Newman) 2. Functioning subgroup in many parts of society (Breen)	1. Overrepresented in some power positions (Atchley; Streib) 2. Dispersed; encompassed within the family system; not functioning as an independent subgroup (Barron; Streib) 3. Lack of distinctive cultural traits (Streib)
Differential Treatment 1. Objects of prejudice and stereotyping (Breen; Palmore) 2. Economic deprivation (Atchley; Jarvis); discriminatory treatment in general (Palmore 1969); discriminatory treatment in employment practices (Barron; Breen; Jarvis); restrictions on full participation in society (Barron); social and/or physical segregation (Breen; Jarvis) 3. Antidiscrimination legislation paralleling that for ethnic groups; arouse fear, seen as a threat (Barron)	1. Refutation of stereotyping in the vital areas of "work performance" and "appropriate activities" (Streib) 2. Deprivation (poverty, unemployment) does not characterize only the old; no restricted access to power, privilege, and rights; minimal involuntary residential segregation; social isolation may be class-related (Streib) 3. Discrimination is situational (Atchley)
Group Consciousness Awareness 1. Negative self-concept (Atchley; Breen; Gubrium; Jarvis; Palmore) 2. Group identification, increasing group consciousness, increasingly likely to organize (Breen; Jarvis; Palmore) 3. Group consciousness not necessary, organization not a requirement (Gubrium)	1. Variability in self-definition of agedness (Streib) 2. Lack of group identification, no consciousness of kind, lack of readiness to organize (Streib)

SOURCE: Published in S. Abu-Laban and B. Abu-Laban, *Aging in Canada: Social Perspectives*, edited by Victor W. Marshall, pp. 63–79 at p. 70 (Don Mills, Ontario: Fitzhenry & Whiteside, 1980).

minority status has been treated as an attribute rather than as a variable in which some groups could be farther or closer to minority status than others. Equating the aged with minority groups has further difficulties in the study of aging in Canada and specifically in the context of aging and ethnicity. The study of ethnic groups in Canada has not focused exclusively or even primarily on those that could be considered minority groups.

This problem is also inherent in the study of the double and multiple jeopardy hypotheses. As noted by Markides (1983), these hypotheses also derive from stratification theory, since they argue that there is interaction between two or more strata, such as age and ethnicity. Jeopardy studies usually concentrate on the combined effects of two or more negatively perceived statuses, such as age and ethnicity, or age, sex, and ethnicity, or age, sex, ethnicity, and social class. Scholars argue that occupying two or more stigmatized statuses has greater negative consequences for the occupants than occupying one negative status alone (Dowd and Bengtson 1978; Palmore and Manton 1973; J. J. Jackson 1972). According to this perspective, being old, female, and a member of a minority group would be worse than being old, female, and not a member of a minority group. A contrary argument is the age as leveller hypothesis, which suggests that age levels everyone's experience to a common (usually low) denominator. Being old is just as bad for a man as it is for a woman. Being old is equally bad whether you are Ukrainian, German, or British.

While the double and multiple jeopardy hypotheses have received much attention, empirical support has been mixed. As Markides (1983) has noted, empirical support is usually reported for traditional indicators used within the stratification literature indicating power, privilege, and prestige (such as income, education, and occupation). However, support in terms of such variables as life satisfaction and primary-group interaction has not been as evident.

This discrepancy is frequently explained in terms of a reference-group effect. Objective inequalities do not translate to the social-psychological level, because we assess our own situation relative to the situation of others whom we use as a basis of comparison. If those relevant to us are no better off or are worse off, we are more likely to be satisfied with our own situation, however disadvantaged by objective indicators or in comparison with those with whom we do not consider it appropriate to compare ourselves. The ethnic factor potentially has much importance in terms of whom we consider our reference group and the value we assign to different statuses.

Discrepancies between objective indicators of disadvantage and studies of the life satisfaction or morale of the elderly suggest the importance of such intervening factors. For example, the Canada Health Survey reveals that approximately 80 percent of elderly persons (those aged 65 and over) in Canada have one or more chronic conditions, about 50 percent have some functional disability, and about 20 percent have a major disability (Health and Welfare Canada and Statistics Canada 1981, as reported in Chappell et al. 1986). However, studies reporting perceptions of health among the elderly suggest only about 25 to 30 percent consider their health to be fair or poor, 70 to 75 percent consider it to be good or excellent (Wolinsky 1983; Chappell et al. 1986). Similarly, measures of life satisfaction or morale suggest small proportions of the elderly report low overall subjective well-being (around 10 percent), with many more at the positive end of the continuum (30 to 50 percent). The role of ethnic identity in the perception by the elderly of their quality of life has not received much attention, especially in Canada. Later in this book the potential importance of this factor for elderly Canadians is discussed in more detail. We turn first, however, to a discussion of modernization theory in aging.

COWGILL'S MODERNIZATION MODEL

The modernization theory of aging argues that the societal process of modernization leads to a progressive decline in the status and social integration of old people. According to Cowgill (1974, 127), modernization is the transformation of a total society from a relatively rural way of life based on animate power, limited technology, relatively undifferentiated institutions, and parochial and traditional outlook and values to a predominantly urban way of life based on inanimate sources of power, highly developed scientific technology, highly differentiated institutions matched by segmented individual roles, and a cosmopolitan outlook that emphasizes efficiency and progress.

In their book *Aging and Modernization*, Cowgill and Holmes (1972) develop 22 discrete propositions correlating pairs of variables. To summarize:

> Modernization is declared to be associated with later onset of old age, increased use of chronological criteria, increased longevity, an aging population, increased proportions of females and widows in the population, increased proportions of grandparents, lower status of the aged, decline in leadership roles of the aged, decline in power and influence of the aged, increased ambiguity of the role of widows and an increase in the extent of disengagement of older people from community life. [Cowgill 1974, 123]

These associations need to be examined and discussed more thoroughly. To help in the discussion of modernization, Cowgill (1974) has isolated four of the most significant and salient changes in modern society that, according to modernization theory, affect the conditions of older people: (1) scientific technology, (2) urbanization, (3) literacy and mass education, and (4) health technology as presented in his model in Figure 2.1. These four modernization processes are discussed next.

FIGURE 2.1
AGING AND MODERNIZATION

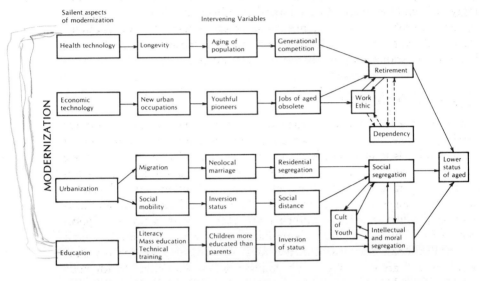

SOURCE: From D. O. Cowgill, "Aging and Modernization: A Revision of the Theory," in J. F. Gubrium (ed.), *Late Life*, p. 141 (1974). Courtesy of Charles C. Thomas, Publisher, Springfield, Illinois.

Health Technology

According to modernization theory, one of the benefits of modern technology is that research has greatly expanded. The theory argues that mortality, because of improved treatment of some diseases, has been lowered, so that a greater percentage of the population now reaches the age of maturity. This has taken place dramatically in the West, where health technology has also resulted in longevity of life. The average adult lives more than 70 years, compared to 40 or 50 years in developing countries. As outlined by Cowgill in Figure 2.1, this has set in motion a sequence leading from health technology, to longevity, to an aging population. Until recently, Canada represented a young population, but more than 9 percent in 1981 were 65 years or older, and this will increase considerably in the future. Urbanization and modernization also lead eventually to a decline in birth rates, so that fewer children are born while the adults live longer, skewing the age of the population increasingly upward (Kalbach and McVey 1979).

Cowgill (1974, 130) suggests that this shift toward an older population inevitably results in competition by the generations for jobs, so that older people are pushed out of the labour market. This has resulted in urban societies institutionalizing a retirement age. In modern society, the work ethic is deeply engrained, and since capitalism is based on the profit motive, employers are always anxious to employ young, strong workers. Since good living is related to an adequate income, many elderly find it increasingly difficult to maintain their standard of living when they no longer work in the paid labour market. Since social status is related to occupational status, retirement removes the older person out of the status market, resulting in lower status and, in many cases, dependency.

Economic Technology

This sequence leads to new urban occupations where youthful pioneers excel and some jobs of older adults become obsolete. The retirement of older adults is therefore desirable. Increased application of inanimate sources of power, reliance on new inventions in agricultural and industrial production, transportation, communication, and distribution all lead to profound changes in the work world. Farmers on the Canadian prairies now have air-conditioned cabins on their large tractors, with radios and upholstered seats. The rise of the computer industry illustrates how specialization and professionalization call for new jobs, for which older workers must retrain if they are to compete with younger people who have already been introduced to this emerging technology in school (Cowgill 1974, 131). Secretaries at most Canadian universities have shifted to word processors. Computers have entered the Canadian scene in most businesses and companies. Increased bureaucratization, proliferation of special interest associations, impersonalization of relationships, and increased interdependence of workers and employers introduce a new dimension to social relationships that is difficult to integrate in later life.

Youth have the advantage in training for and adapting to new urban occupations, which emerge ever more rapidly on the economic scene. Labour unions are trying to slow the pace of technological change in the postal service, in factories, and the like, but such innovations are escalating so that modernization is difficult to stop. Youth are also more mobile, seeking new frontiers geographically as well as occupationally. In many cases older parents find themselves in less prestigious, more static, occupations. Older people are often deprived of providing vocational guidance and instruction to their children.

Urbanization

Cowgill (1974) suggests two aspects of urbanization (geographical and social mobility) that affect the status of old age. In rural areas, there is a tendency for the youth to move to the city, leaving the elderly behind on the farms or in small towns. Henry's (1973) Vale Haven blacks in Nova Scotia are a good example. Frideres's (1983) discussion of native urbanization suggests the same. Small villages or towns may be located in heavily ethnic areas where the elderly are relatively close to many familiar ethnic opportunities. However, when many of their children or grandchildren move farther away to cities, residential segregation becomes greater. Such residential segregation, linked with separation of nuclear families into neolocal patterns, enhances the likelihood of social segregation and therefore lower status for the aged. This places heavy strains upon the extended family, resulting in spatial separation of the generations. Even telephone advertisements now advise us to call friends and kin more. Weekly visits into town, or across town in cities, are not as easy, so that the frequency and intimacy of contact suffers. Distance between residences of family members also mitigates against immediate availability. That is, modernization theory suggests less cohesive, less supportive family bonds.

Urbanization not only induces geographic mobility, it also accelerates social mobility. The young are more open to change than the old are and have less to lose by trying new opportunities. Cowgill (1974, 134) suggests that children consciously or unconsciously feel superior to their parents because they are familiar with the latest trends. More youth move to the city, the city encourages a more modern lifestyle, and the new and modern promotes higher prestige. When these urbanites visit the country, they tend to feel that they are more sophisticated than their parents. In this sense there is a social distance and an inversion of social status, because the rural elderly are isolated and segregated socially.

Education

Premodern societies depend largely on oral tradition, so the aged have an important role in perpetuating and interpreting past traditions. The elderly act as a repository of the past in a preliterate environment. This is still the case in northern aboriginal settings, and to some extent on farms. With urbanization and formal education, literacy, mass education, and technical training are necessary. Children are often more educated than their parents, especially in the beginning stages of the modernization process. Thus the elderly do not have a monopoly on knowledge. Indeed, youth have the advantage, because they have more opportunities to obtain more recent knowledge through formal education, which in certain fields, and sometimes in general, results in an inversion of educational status.

Training programs in technical knowledge are directed more to the young, and they have first exposure to new trends. They also have access to the latest in communication to compete for jobs. Modernization tends to bring about change and new trends, which stimulate a need to evaluate ethnic, religious, and traditional values. It is for this reason that Cowgill suggests that intellectual and moral segregation take place between the generations. "The cult of youth" is more valued than old age, because it is more efficient and more progressive; the modern and the new are more esteemed. Since youth are usually more open to recent change, there can be conflict and misunderstanding between the elderly and the succeeding generations.

Criticisms

Modernization theory has come under close scrutiny. Both Fischer (1978) and Laslett (1976) argue it assumes a universal golden age for the elderly in the past. Both demonstrate the empirical falsity of such a nostalgic view of the past. The elderly in past times were not necessarily revered.

Others have assessed the model through comparisons of different societies and report a variety of findings. Palmore and Manton (1973) studied 31 countries in various stages of modernization (using indicators of economic technology, urbanization, and education). They found that those societies that were more modern, according to occupation and education indicators, accorded relatively high status to their elderly. In response, Cowgill (1974) argues that the detrimental effects to the status and interests of the aged in the early period of modernization may "bottom out" in later periods.

Bengtson et al. (1975) tested the theory in a comparative study of over 5,000 adults in six developing nations (Argentina, Chile, India, Israel, Nigeria, and Bangladesh) to see whether there was an association between modernity and negative attitudes toward aging. Their findings are mixed, and the authors conclude there is no consistent support for a simple relation between increasing negative views of the aged and increasing modernity. Evidence suggesting negative views of old age in the pre-Christian and early Christian era (circa 3,000 B.C.–1,300 A.D.) and high esteem for the elderly in some modern societies such as Japan and Ireland further contradict the theory (Hendricks and Hendricks 1977; Palmore 1975; Rhoads 1984).

In his historical account of growing old in America, Fischer (1978) reviews studies relevant to the modernizaton theory. His finding is important. He concludes that every recent study of aging since the 1940s disagrees with the modernization model in one way or another, that studies before World War II agree with the modernization model, and that those in the postmodern era (1945 to the present) report the reverse of the hypotheses. To illustrate this reverse effect, it has been found that income levels for the elderly are higher than they were (Schulz 1976) and that technological advances and increased productivity raise the standards of living for many, including the elderly (Hauser 1976).

However some, like Dowd (1980), argue that despite the exceptions, modernization theory is valid. Dowd (1980) argues that the exceptions appear to contradict the theory only because the explanatory or organizing principles have not been general enough. He sees himself as increasing the scope of modernization theory by drawing on the theory of exchange. The distribution of power resources among competing groups is considered the major determinant of exchange rates, where power is a function of privilege, not necessarily of the individual's or group's relation to the means of production. The relative power of the aged vis-à-vis the society increasingly deteriorates, so that an imbalanced exchange ratio results, forcing many aged to trade compliance, their last resource, for societal sustenance.

According to exchange theory, people tend to choose courses of action from among a known range of alternatives on the basis of anticipated outcomes (Lipman 1982, 195). The goal of exchange is to maximize rewards and reduce costs (Homans 1961). Interaction will usually continue as long as the exchange is perceived as more rewarding than costly. Power enters in when one participant gains more from the exchange than the other; one of the individuals can no longer reciprocate equally. Impaired health, depleted income, and/or loss of a spouse are all partially responsible for decreased social interaction of the elderly. Whereas a worker was able to exchange expertise for needed wages, the retired person must comply with mandatory retirement in exchange for sustenance (social security, medicare, etc.) (Dowd 1980).

In modern industrial society, with its demand for current knowledge and technological innovation, the skills of many aged persons quickly become outmoded; hence, the bargaining position of the retired person quickly deteriorates as his or her supply of power resources becomes depleted. The aged of preindustrial society were more able than the aged of today to accumulate a large share of power resources, largely due to expertise gained from a life of living in a much more stable society.

When the exchange relation becomes unbalanced, equilibrium can be restored through four balancing operations: withdrawal, extension of the power network, emergence of status, and coalition formation. Withdrawal is a form of disengagement where less is received and therefore less demanded in return. The power network can be extended by developing new roles for the aged (this is often advocated by activity theorists), so that additional sources of rewarding behaviour are available. Formerly valued skills could be revived, or new skills found that could result in emergence of status. Coalition of the aged with younger persons could help both to build on their skills by combining strengths. It will be seen later that some authors argue that specialized ethnic knowledge can be viewed as a previously untapped power source for the ethnic elderly.

Cowgill (1974) himself has responded to criticisms of modernization theory with four modifications: (1) the work ethic may be softening, so that not working in old age is less of a disgrace; (2) after a society reaches a certain stage of affluence, it is willing to provide for nonproductive citizens; (3) when illiteracy disappears, the aged handicap also lessens; and (4) self-awareness among the elderly may grow within modernization and result in the elderly applying political pressure to attain their rights. These writers suggest that modernization theory, like all theories, has its limitations.

Modifications

One of the major criticisms of modernization theory that has led to modifications in thinking about the place of old people in society is the very concept of status used by Cowgill and Holmes (1972). Goldstein and Beall (1981) and Rhoads (1984) argue that the use of high prestige and social standing for high status is misleading. These authors work with eight separate components of status: biology, health, activity, authority, economics, household, psychology, and ritual. Conceptualizing status in terms of prestige means the status of the aged can decline while their health or income or authority or psychological well-being, for example, improves. Rhoads suggests cultural values and ideological orientations may well influence the relation between modernization and status. For example, an emphasis on equality may be responsible for a decline in the status of the aged.

The argument that prestige and social standing, especially as derived from economic status, may not be the only status worth considering, is evident in current (and some not so current) sociological writings. It is interesting to note that Weber, in his many writings on economics, capitalism, bureaucracy, and rationalization, was, in response to the writings of Karl Marx, greatly preoccupied with the place of religion in society. Helle (1985, 198) points out what Weber's last publication prior to his death was his *Sociology of Religion*, in which he paints the modern rational culture with dark colours. The individual trained to strive for rationality constantly intensifies his individuality and self-sufficiency and thereby isolates himself more and more at the cost of a progressive loss of meaning.

Berger (1982, 64) links modernization with secularization and defines *modernization* as a "constellation of institutions and structures of consciousness" founded in technology, the market economy, the contemporary state, bureaucracy, the contemporary city, and mass communication. He (1982, 66) claims that evidence of counter-modernity is found in political socialism, where some individualism is given up in return for real community and more security: it is a dream of the restored middle ages. He suggests the need for a balance between tradition and modernity in which both freedom and security reside in tension with each other.

Horowitz (1982) follows the same theme as Weber and Berger, suggesting that the "new fundamentalism" among the Muslims in the Arab world, and the conservative religious and political trends in the United States, are counter-modern movements in quest of more security. He suggests that the various forms of socialism and communism are a revolt against individualist capitalism. The secular traditions, including the French Enlightenment,

German enlightenment and romanticism, and American modernism, have all experienced a crisis, one he refers to as a system overload. Each generation confronts so much information, digests so much material, absorbs so much innovation, and stores so much scientific knowledge that there is overload and a concomitant tendency to disgorge or empty out (Horowitz 1982, 47). All of these authors argue that there is a counter-modernization trend evident in society in which economic status becomes devalued.

Modernization and Ethnicity

As Rosenthal (1983) has noted, high ethnic-identity families are assumed to fall at the traditional end of a traditional-modern continuum. In general, the ethnic family is characterized by respect for elderly members, a high degree of familism, cohesion, and continuity between the generations, providing much support and integration for their aged members. This is contrasted with the white or Anglo-Saxon (supposedly non-ethnic) family, which is assumed to fall at the modern end of the continuum.

A recognition that this assumption may be false is also clearly evident. As Mitchell and Register (1984) discuss in relation to blacks, two conflicting descriptions are evident in the literature. One views the black aged as being at the centre of an extended family network that provides social and material support. The other views blacks as adjusting to a family system changing from traditional to middle-class roles, characterized by losses in interaction between the generations. In a similar vein, Markides et al. (1986) note that earlier studies of the Mexican American family argue for the protective and supportive nature of family relationships. However, the 1960s saw a recognition of over-romanticizing the place of Mexican American elderly in the family and the need for empirical research in the area.

As Holzberg (1981) suggests, ethnicity should not necessarily be subsumed under a traditional designation, but should be introduced as a variable to differentiate ethnic cultural patterns. Ethnic identity and interaction may help to sustain cultural patterns (language, symbols, norms, institutions). The British elderly can be sustained by their cultural familiarity, and the Jewish elderly may also maintain a meaningful Jewish identity. Both groups could be more modern than traditional types. It is a fallacy to treat all ethnic elderly the same (as traditional or modern types). Modernization theory tends to pose a static view of culture that is too simplistic. Ethnic elderly must be studied comparatively, and we must assume that there is a pool of meaning in each ethnic culture, from which many draw, not always in a similar way. Thus, the salience of ethnic identity within each group may vary, as may patterns of behaviour with respect to different cultural variables. These patterns may vary over time and across cultures, for example, native Indians or Japanese in Canada and the United States.

Similarly, exchange theory has tended to present an overly simplistic and static view of the elderly. Within this perspective, the problems of the elderly are generally seen as ones of decreasing power resources and of differential values placed on resources by older persons. Those using exchange theory tend to view the balance of power in favour of the younger person. However, as Cool (1981) argues, one could view an older ethnic person as possessing resources valued by the younger person and in favour of the older person. The older ethnic person has both expressive knowledge (family anecdotes and kinship information that provide a sense of history and belonging) and instrumental knowledge (of old ways of life in the homeland) of interest to younger members of the group as evidence of their cultural distinctiveness. Cool (1981) studied the Corsicans in France and the Portuguese in California and concluded that elderly persons did take advantage of younger people's interest in their knowledge of the old ways. Ethnicity provided the elderly with a source of identity and a previously unexploited power resource.

Assumptions about the linking of ethnic families with a traditional way of life and the argument that elderly people in modern society experience a decrease in power resources share some similarities with assumptions in assimilation theory. Popular for some 50 years in ethnic studies, especially in the United States, assimilation theory also perpetuates deterministic features of evolution similar to those found in modernization theory. That literature is now reviewed and the assumptions for the ethnic elderly discussed. Similarities between the aging literature and the ethnicity literature are examined.

PARK'S ASSIMILATION THEORY

A chief advocate of the process of ethnic assimilation was Robert Park, who suggested that when immigrants entered America and came into contact with society, they took either the route of least resistance (contact, accommodation, assimilation) or a more circuitous route (contact, conflict, competition, accommodation, fusion) (see Hughes 1950). This theory is an evolutionary approach in that it assumes that all ethnic groups will change, losing their original language, culture, and values, and adopting the values, norms, and structures of their host society. In North America this is assumed to be Anglo-Celtic. The question for assimilationists is not whether these minorities will assimilate, but how fast. Nor is there a question about the focus or direction to which such groups move: they move toward the majority group. Park did not develop the theory to distinguish between the cultural and structural, although others such as Gordon (1964) did (see below).

There is evidence that in Canadian history many British leaders and influentials had the Anglo-conformity model in mind when they thought of the aboriginal people, the French, and other immigrants. Lord Durham assumed that others would assimilate to a British legal, linguistic, political, economic, and cultural system (Stanley 1963). Many seem to have hoped that somehow even the French would finally assimilate, although via Park's circuitous route of conflict and competition. While some may have desired assimilation, it has not in fact happened for many.

Today it is less popular than earlier to express the Anglo-conformity and assimilationist perspective, but Porter (1979) did pursue such views to some extent. Porter referred to ethnicity and multiculturalism as *primordial identity*. He tended to emphasize the overwhelming influence of technology and urbanization as the master trend that sweeps away all forms of ethnic differentiation before it. Vallee says:

> There is no doubt that Porter would have rejoiced had ethnic differentiation disappeared altogether. ... If a choice had to be made between the ideology of the melting pot and the mosaic, he made it clear he would choose the melting pot. What bothered Porter more than anything was that these group or collective rights were ascriptive, that is determined by the categories into which one was born. [Vallee 1981, 641]

In his *Vertical Mosaic*, Porter (1965) argued that ethnicity was an impediment to upward social mobility, and he was concerned that all should have the maximum chance to better themselves socioeconomically. Here Porter's deterministic assumption of assimilation is clear. However, numerous scholars (Breton 1984; Darroch 1979; Tepperman 1975) show that this linkage is not as clear as Porter claimed. These studies show that for some groups, like the Jews, Chinese, and Mennonites, ethnicity is not an impediment for mobility (Reitz 1982).

It is true that for many of north European origin, who are similar culturally and racially (such as the Scandinavians, Dutch, and Germans), a shift to English home language use is common and cultural distinctions are declining. This is less true for the elderly than for younger generations. The aboriginal elderly, French Canadians, Hutterites, and many visible minorities such as blacks, East and West Indians, and Asians have not assimilated but have either voluntarily or involuntarily retained their identity (Driedger 1975; Isajiw and Makabe 1982). Many of these ethnic identifiers among old-age groups remain in conflict and have not automatically assimilated in due course, as many assimilationists predicted. Jews have maintained their identity in many countries for thousands of years, blacks in the United States and aboriginals in North America for hundreds of years.

Multicultural Pluralism: The Ethnic Mosaic

While counter-modernization voices on aging are only beginning to be heard, multicultural, plural counter-assimilation arguments in ethnicity have developed very strongly. In Canada, pluralism is becoming more popular than assimilation. Proponents argue that many groups retain a separate identity and do not assimilate; they live side by side, many of them in relatively harmonious coexistence. The author of this view of pluralism was a Harvard educated philosopher of Jewish immigrant stock named Kallen. In 1924, he argued that while there are many kinds of social relationships and identities that can be chosen voluntarily, no one may choose his or her ancestry (see Newman 1973). Kallen argued that each of the minority groups has something of value to contribute to a country, and that the American Constitution carries with it an implicit assumption that all people are created equal, even though there might be many distinct differences.

In contrast to assimilation, which emphasizes technology and urbanization as the major forces of influence, cultural pluralism focuses on countervailing forces of ideology, such as democracy and human justice, which teach that all people are of equal worth and all should have the freedom to choose their quality and style of life. Pluralism holds that there is greater resistance to assimilate than had formerly been thought. This pluralist trend has already taken place in the political arena, where numerous political parties are considered desirable, as well as in religion, in the various forms of religious adherence since the Protestant reformation. If pluralism works in politics and religion, why should it not also be acceptable to exercise cultural pluralism?

In Canada, especially, the French, the first European settlers who constitute a sizeable group (26 percent in 1981), have been impossible to assimilate. They are highly concentrated in Quebec, where they have political control provincially. The aboriginal people in the Northlands of Canada represent a majority of tiles in the ethnic mosaic in that part of the country. Canada's blacks, Jews, Hutterites, Doukhobours, Asians, and many others such as the Italians and Jews in major cities and the Ukrainians and Germans in prairie bloc settlements, add to the linguistic and cultural mosaic of a plural Canada. While some of these have assimilated more than others, many have retained distinctive identities. When Trudeau, in 1971, declared Canada a multicultural society in a bilingual framework, he provided a further boost to pluralism in Canada. Even in the United States, most current writings in ethnicity and aging adopt a cultural pluralism perspective, assuming significant differences between groups.

Modifications of the Ideal Polarities

It is obvious that the two polarities, assimilation and pluralism, represent opposite ideal polar types and that some ethnic groups lean more toward one than the other along a continuum between the two poles. Elderly Indians in the north, the French aged in rural Quebec, and Hutterites on the prairies lean toward the pluralist pole, while many Icelanders in Manitoba and the Dutch and German elderly in cities have assimilated enormously. However, there are many who are some of both, so it is necessary to look at three modifications — modified assimilation, modified pluralism, and conflict — which illustrate the complexity of change and adjustments that take place.

Gordon (1964) suggests that assimilation is not only one process but many cultural and structural subprocesses. Thus, he favours a modified assimilation perspective. Cultural assimilation includes acceptance by the incoming group of modes of dress, language, attitudes, and other cultural characteristics of the host society. Structural assimilation has to do with the degree to which immigrants enter the economic, political, religious, educational, welfare, and social institutions of society and the degree to which they are accepted by the host society. Gordon suggests that the opposing processes of assimilation and pluralism may take place simultaneously, depending on which dimension of ethnic activity is examined. Newman (1973) points out that "once structural assimilation is far advanced, all other types of assimilation will naturally follow."

Gordon (1964) examined seven dimensions of change: cultural, structural, marital, identificational, civic, and attitudinal and behavioural receptional forms of assimilation. He assumed that each of these seven was a subprocess of its own and that each would develop at a pace of its own. In some subprocesses assimilation and disappearance into the host society might be almost complete, while in other subprocesses plural distinctiveness might remain. Thus, each can be thought of as falling on a continuum with the two opposite polarities, pluralism and assimilation.

Cultural assimilation has to do with loss of language and dress and with distinctive cultural changes in attitudes and norms of filial obligation, and the like, while structural assimilation involves movement from ethnic schools, churches, and social organizations to host institutions. Exogamy represents marital assimilation; identificational change involves physical visibility such as different races; and civic change has to do with influence in the political arena. Prejedice and discrimination would be good substitutes for the two forms of receptional assimilation. While the other five subprocesses involve the minorities themselves, the extent to which such minorities are received by the majority (favourable or unfavourable attitudes and behaviour) has to do with the degree of acceptance minorities find in the host society.

What is important about Gordon's seven subprocesses is that he allows for many dimensions of change, so that in some subprocesses more assimilation takes place, while in other subprocesses more ethnic identity is maintained. Thus, Gordon's modified assimilation perspective helps to take into account much more of the complexity of both the assimilation and pluralism processes.

While Gordon suggests a modification of assimilation theory, Glazer and Moynihan (1963) elaborate a modification of the pluralism perspective.

They distinguish four major events in New York City history involving the Jews, Irish Catholics, blacks and Puerto Ricans. The large number of Jews in New York and their support of the new state of Israel and Zionism provided enormous issues for Jewish identification. The Irish Catholic controversy over Catholic schools and their drive for religious education gave them a focus for identity. The influx of visible minorities of blacks and Puerto Ricans illustrated ethnic residential segregation and led to latent prejudice and discrimination, which enhanced pluralism rather than assimilation.

Glazer and Moynihan's point was that religion, race, and culture are salient ethnic factors that did not melt easily in the melting pot. While the blacks might have wished to assimilate, they were not allowed to; and the Jews did not want to assimilate, because of the distinctive religion that was important to them. Voluntary and involuntary forms of pluralism are well illustrated in New York. Over time these various ethnic groups may change, but they do not disappear into the larger society. Rather, they take on distinctly new modified pluralist religious, cultural, or physical forms (eg., generational differences).

A third form of modification of the polar assimilation and pluralism perspective is represented in conflict theory. One way to view conflict is the classic Marxian dialectical form, the struggle between two classes, the bourgeoisie and the proletariat. Thus, conflict between various ethnic or age groups could be postulated; a struggle between elderly people and the rest of society for social status, for power and prestige. Most ethnic groups do not conduct such extensive power struggles, although the FLQ movement in Quebec might be a good example of one that did. Similar struggles take place in Northern Ireland between the Protestants and Catholics, in the Near East between Israel and many Arabs, and recently between blacks and whites in South Africa. The Parti Québécois can be seen as a milder form of conflict institution, which sought to gain sovereign control of Quebec's economic, political, and social institutions by a referendum to secede.

While power conflict may occasionally take the form of revolution and secession, it is also present in lesser forms (Coser 1956). When many subgroups and a multitude of cultures exist side by side, they maintain distinct identities, thus providing a potential for conflict of values, territorial interests, and power relations. J. D. Jackson (1975) saw such a French-English struggle in Windsor, Ontario in schools and in the community where the French were a minority. The French language question in Manitoba recently brought forth a similar emotional conflict, which the courts were asked to referee. By the same token, Quebec's Quiet Revolution, the native peoples' quest for land rights, and the relations between adjacent ethnic prairie communities, all demonstrate a constant potential for dissension. Hutterite expansion into the Alberta farmlands and the subsequent passing of restrictive legislation, and the conflict between Italians and the Quebec province over the language Bill 101, are examples of countercultural ethnic conflicts (Hostetler and Huntington 1967; Richmond 1972).

In summary, it is clear that while the two polar perspectives of assimilation and pluralism are useful ways to view ethnic change, they tend to be ideal types. While some groups may be moving toward assimilation or pluralism, the perspectives must often be modified because both tendencies may be present in the same phenomenon. Thus, the various modifications of Gordon, Moynihan and Glazer, and Marx all contribute to a better understanding of the complexity of social change. This was also true in our discussion of the various theories and forms of modernization. These two traditions of theoretical thought must now be examined to see whether there are any similarities, or in what way these two fields of study in aging and ethnicity interface.

TOWARD A THEORETICAL INTERFACE BETWEEN AGING AND ETHNICITY

In Figure 2.2 the modernization and assimilation theories dominant in their respective aging and ethnicity fields are plotted. After having discussed each of the two, some striking similarities as well as some differences can be observed. There is a great need to integrate the two fields of ethnicity and aging; this will provide the opportunity to see whether there is an interface between the two, where overlap and diversity lie. Essentially the question becomes, with increased modernization, do the elderly lose status, and to what extent does this vary by ethnicity? To what extent do various ethnic groups assimilate or retain their identity, and how does this affect the elderly? What is the relation between modernization and assimilation, and what are the consequences for the elderly?

First, both master trends (modernization and assimilation) begin with a solid base of tradition or an "ethnos" (see Figure 2.2). We think of modernization beginning in a folk or rural area that has not yet become urbanized. Here family solidarity, security, and stability are the norm, often segregated in ethnic enclaves where culture, language, and symbolism are fairly stable. With limited change, modest education, and food-gathering or food-producing occupations, differentiation among members of the community is also on a small scale. Thus, it is easier for the elderly to retain a valued place where social nearness is common and differentiation of labour and retirement are fairly informal.

Second, while modernization trends are much in evidence, the deterministic evolutionary goal of increasing progress must be further examined. Our discussion of modernization does not concede that economic social status is necessarily the main determinant of status. In addition, many elderly retain power. This is most evident in the political (Reagan,

FIGURE 2.2

MODERNIZATION AND ASSIMILATION PROCESSES AND GOALS

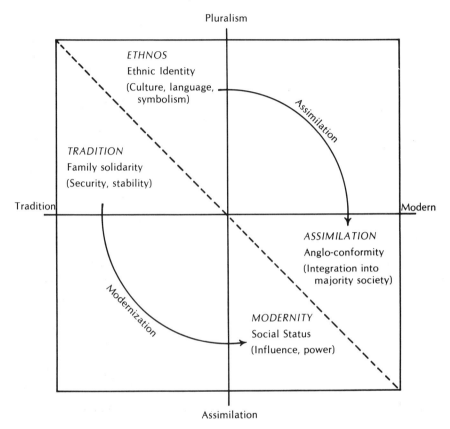

Breshnev) and economic (Rockefeller, Vanderbilt) arenas. Demographic trends leading to increasing proportions of elderly could be a major factor in the future.

Third, it must not be assumed that as modernization increases, ethnic assimilation will necessarily follow. As discussed in the next chapter, the Jews and Chinese, who retain high degrees of ethnic identity, are also among the more urbanized, educated, and professional groups. Assimilating into the larger whole does not happen to many distinct groups, for both voluntary and involuntary reasons. There is considerable evidence that ethnic identity survives for many generations. While assimilation and Anglo-conformity may happen to some, it does not happen to all. This leaves many unassimilated ethnic elderly of various groups, who will have distinctive linguistic, cultural, religious, and social needs. This will be addressed in more detail later.

SUMMARY

Both the modernization and assimilation theories tend to be too linear, not taking sufficient account of multivariate trends. Which factors, such as disengagement, activity, exchange, technology, urbanization, and education are in operation, when, and to what extent? The multivariate approach emphasizes the reality of a variety of places and different groups. The various modifications of assimilation and pluralism, taking into account social conflict, have also demonstrated that many cultural, structural, marital, civic, identificational, prejudicial, and discriminatory factors must be considered. The strengths of multivariate analyses seem apparent.

The theories of modernization in the field of aging and assimilation in the study of ethnicity are too deterministic in stating loss of status and loss of identity, respectively. Greater allowance must be made for multivariate processes, which often modify as well as contradict their master theses. Life satisfaction may be more important than economic status for the elderly, and ethnic identity is still an important factor for many in the Canadian mosaic. In Chapter 3 we explore the extent to which assimilation and modernization affect the ethnic elderly in Canada. In Chapter 4 we explore the relevance of primary group relations for the role of eth-elders within various ethnic groups.

CHAPTER 3

THE ETHNIC FACTOR

Some of the general demographic characteristics underlying the social structure of the ethnic elderly were outlined in Chapter 1, and some of the major theoretical underpinnings of studies in aging and in ethnicity were reviewed in Chapter 2. We now turn to a discussion of empirical evidence of modernization and assimilation. Available data are few.

ETHNIC ELDERLY AND SOCIAL CHANGE

Cowgill's (1974) four salient aspects of modernization — education, urbanization, economic technology, and health technology — will be discussed first using empirical data. To examine assimilation, we shall concentrate on indicators of ethnic pluralism such as use of ethnic language and the religious orientation of the ethnic elderly. The extent of modernization and assimilation among the ethnic groups is expected to vary significantly, so it can be assumed that the needs of their elderly will vary as well.

Education as a Form of Modernization

As age increases, the educational level of Canadians decreases (Statistics Canada 1981). Most younger adults (age 25–64) have some high school education or better (80 percent), while two-thirds (62 percent) of the elderly 85 years and older have less than grade nine. This suggests that with time the level of education for the elderly will rise as the younger, more educated adults age. In the meantime, planners must remember that they are dealing with a majority of elderly who have formal education of elementary school level. Does this vary by ethnicity, so that working with different ethnic groups might call for varied needs based on levels of education?

A more careful look at the various ethnic groups in Table 3.1 shows that proportionately more of the Jews (3.4 percent), Chinese (1.2 percent), and British (56.2 percent) compared with other ethnic elderly (aged 55 plus) hold a bachelor's degree. Jews in particular have three times (3.4 percent) as many with bachelor's degrees as their proportion (1.1 percent) of the population. On the other hand, the Portuguese (2 percent) have five times as many and the Italians (8.6 percent) more than three times as many with below grade five education. In addition, the Ukrainians (6.5 percent), Poles (2.8 percent), and French (37.7 percent) have disproportionate numbers

TABLE 3.1

EDUCATION LEVEL OF CANADA'S ELDERLY (55 YEARS AND OVER) BY ETHNIC GROUPS

Ethnic Origin	% of Total Canadian Population	Educational Level				
		Less than Grade 5	Grade 5-8	Grade 9-13	High School Graduate	B.A. Degree or more
British	45.4	20.8	38.1	62.1	50.0	56.2
French	23.2	37.7	31.8	14.1	29.9	16.2
African	.2	.3	.1	.2	.2	.2
Chinese	.7	2.6	.5	.5	.6	1.2
Dutch	1.5	.8	1.9	1.2	1.1	1.2
German	5.1	4.0	6.6	4.9	3.1	3.8
Greek	.3	.7	.4	.2	.1	.2
Italian	2.5	8.6	3.2	1.2	1.2	.5
Jewish	1.1	1.5	1.1	2.3	2.8	3.4
Polish	1.7	2.8	2.2	1.3	.9	1.4
Portuguese	.4	2.0	.2	.1	.1	.1
Scandinavian	1.7	.6	1.8	2.1	1.1	1.8
Ukrainian	3.1	6.5	3.9	2.7	1.6	1.8
Other Single	4.1	8.3	4.3	3.6	3.6	5.8
Other	9.0	2.8	3.9	3.6	3.7	5.0
Total	100.0	100.0	100.0	100.0	100.0	100.0

SOURCE: Derived from the 2% Public Census Tape obtained from the Canadian Association on Gerontology/Association Canadienne de Gerontologie.

with below grade five education. Interestingly, the Chinese (2.6 percent) have four times as many with less than a grade five education, even though they also have twice as many with bachelor's degrees. That is, they represent a bimodal tendency.

It is quite clear that ethnicity is an important factor in differentiating the Canadian population by education. It is likely that other factors cluster with the educated and non-educated poles, supporting the notion of ethnic polar types. Dealing with the Portuguese and Italian elderly probably requires very different skills and insights than working with the more educated Jewish and British elderly. The bimodal Chinese have significant numbers of uneducated, bachelor males who immigrated some time ago as well as educated, professional elderly who immigrated recently, which indicates a range of diversity within one ethnic group.

Urbanism as Modernization

Our analysis so far suggests that the Jewish elderly are the most educated, and they also have the highest proportion (16.5 percent) who are over age

65. On the other hand, Canada's native peoples illustrate the reverse pattern in that they are the least educated and have the lowest proportion (3.5 percent) who are over 65. We expect that most Jews reside in urban areas and that the majority of native peoples live in rural areas. Is this the case?

In Table 3.2, ten of the largest metropolitan areas in Canada are analyzed to examine the extent of ethnic urbanization, and variations among the ethnic groups. Natives are not shown here, but rural segregation is common, with the native peoples scattered very heavily in the Northlands where it is difficult to provide services, much as they need them. A. B. Anderson (1972) has demonstrated how the Germans, Dutch, Scandinavians, and Ukrainians are segregated in the prairie bloc settlements on farms. Here the elderly have more opportunity to fight the encroaching forms of modernization, which modernization theorists would argue bring about a lowering of status, because many can continue to farm, although at a slower pace, by letting some of their children do the farming. At the same time, many are sufficiently well-to-do that they can either provide for their keep during old age or enter smaller homes in town, often provided by their respective religious groups. Many move into small towns, easily accessible to their children, where they are not too distant from their neighbours and kin.

Occupational Status and Modern Technology

Cowgill (1974) suggested economic technology as a third indicator of modernization and argued that new urban occupations provide evidence of this increased technology. In Table 3.3, 15 categories of occupations are listed, some of them distinctly rural (farming and primary occupations, such as mining, fishing, and forestry) and others clearly more urban (managerial, engineering, clerical, sales). To what extent were Canada's elderly (aged 55 and older) engaged in, or formerly engaged in, these occupations, and are some ethnic origins more heavily represented in some categories?

The British elderly, the largest charter and ethnic group, are overrepresented in the high status occupations (managerial, engineering) and underrepresented in low status, blue collar occupations such as processing, machining, and construction. The reverse is generally true for the French, the other charter group. While the British are very close to the average in farming and primary occupations, the French are underrepresented in farming and overrepresented in other primary occupations. The British elderly are clearly in higher status occupations than the French, although the economic technology indicator of modernization does not correlate clearly with status occupations.

Other ethnic groups tend to cluster in interesting patterns. The Germans, Dutch, Ukrainians, and Scandinavians are overrepresented in farming. These groups are also heavily represented in the Prairie Provinces, while the Jews, Chinese, and Italians are greatly underrepresented. On the other hand, the Jews are greatly overrepresented in sales, managerial, artistic, and

Table 3.2

Percentage of Ethnic Elderly (55 Years and Older) in Ten Metropolitan Centres of Canada, 1981

Ethnic Origin	St. John	Halifax	Quebec	Montreal	Ottawa	Toronto	Kitchener	Winnipeg	Edmonton	Vancouver
British	91.0	73.3	3.7	15.2	48.6	53.8	44.1	40.6	41.7	56.8
French	2.4	8.7	89.4	58.7	30.8	1.8	2.5	6.4	5.5	3.2
Chinese	.1	2.7	.2	.4	.6	1.8	.3	.5	1.8	4.2
Dutch	.1	3.6	.1	.2	.7	1.0	1.8	1.7	2.9	1.3
German	.1	.1	.1	1.2	2.0	3.0	29.3	8.7	8.8	5.7
Italian	.1	.7	.1	5.0	1.9	7.4	.9	1.3	1.2	2.0
Jewish		.3		5.5	1.5	5.6	.2	4.8	.9	.9
Polish				1.1	1.2	2.7	2.8	5.2	3.4	1.6
Portuguese				.4	.3	1.5	2.4	.5	.3	.2
Scandinavian	.2	.3		.1	.4	.4	.3	3.1	4.2	4.2
Ukrainian		.2		1.0	1.1	2.9	2.0	13.7	14.2	2.8
Other Single	1.0	2.4	.7	5.4	3.6	11.9	5.7	7.1	7.3	9.0
Multiple	1.4	4.5	.6	1.7	3.0	2.4	3.6	2.3	2.7	2.8
Other	3.6	3.2	5.1	4.1	4.3	3.8	4.1	4.1	5.1	5.3
Total	100.0	100.0	100.0	100.0	100.0	100.0	100.0	100.0	100.0	100.0

Source: Derived from the 2% Public Census Tape obtained from the Canadian Association on Gerontology/Association Canadienne de Gerontologie.

TABLE 3.3
OCCUPATIONAL STATUS OF ETHNIC GROUPS IN CANADA (AGED 55 AND OVER) IN 1981

	British	French	Chinese	Dutch	German	Italian	Jewish	Polish	Portu-guese	Scand-inavian	Ukrainian	Other Single	Multiple Mixed	N	TOTAL %
Managerial	54.7	18.0	.3	1.5	4.5	1.8	5.3	1.1	.1	1.5	2.5	6.0	2.6	3,452	100
Engineering	55.2	13.5	1.0	3.4	5.0	1.0	1.4	2.6	.1	2.4	1.7	9.3	3.4	765	100
Social Services	56.5	17.1	.0	1.3	5.4	.6	3.6	1.5	.0	1.5	3.2	5.8	3.4	467	100
Teaching	50.6	23.5	.4	2.0	5.9	.8	2.2	1.4	.1	2.0	2.8	6.0	2.4	1,005	100
Health, Med.	53.4	20.6	.3	1.5	4.4	.6	3.1	1.3	.2	.9	2.4	7.2	4.1	1,237	100
Artistic, Ent.	51.6	20.2	.2	2.0	4.2	2.0	4.2	.5	.0	2.0	1.2	8.1	3.3	401	100
Clerical	56.9	18.5	.4	1.2	3.9	1.6	3.0	1.4	.2	1.5	2.7	5.5	3.4	5,090	100
Sales	52.0	18.8	.6	1.8	4.7	1.7	6.1	1.3	.2	1.9	3.0	4.7	2.7	3,502	100
Service	41.3	22.3	.5	1.6	6.0	4.4	.7	3.0	1.1	1.6	5.0	8.5	2.5	4,807	100
Farming	46.3	12.8	.3	3.6	12.3	1.0	.1	2.2	.3	4.3	7.1	8.1	1.8	2,584	100
Primary, other	48.8	31.4	.2	.8	2.5	1.6	.0	2.3	.2	2.0	3.3	11.5	1.4	488	100
Processing	32.6	30.9	.8	1.5	5.8	5.9	1.1	3.5	.8	1.5	4.1	9.3	2.2	1,233	100
Machining	36.0	23.7	.5	1.7	6.8	7.3	1.9	3.8	.7	1.4	3.6	9.8	2.8	3,229	100
Construction	39.3	25.4	.1	3.1	6.8	7.1	.5	1.7	1.1	2.7	3.4	7.2	1.7	2,119	100
Transport	49.8	29.5	.0	1.6	4.2	1.2	1.3	1.5	.2	1.8	2.8	4.4	1.7	1,278	100
Other	42.5	26.6	.6	1.7	4.8	3.9	.5	3.0	.4	1.5	3.8	7.6	2.9	1,877	100
Total % of Population	45.4	23.2	.7	1.5	5.1	2.5	1.7	1.7	.4	1.7	3.1	6.4	2.4	33,534	100

SOURCE: Derived from the 2% Public Census Tape obtained from the Canadian Association on Gerontology/Association Canadienne de Gerontologie.

literary occupations, as well as in social science and health occupations. None of the other ethnic elderly are as heavily engaged as the Jews in these high status, modern forms of work. While the Italians are greatly under-represented in these modern, high status occupations, they, as well as the Polish elderly, are heavily engaged in modern, lower status, blue collar jobs such as machining, construction, processing, and service occupations. The Italians cluster in the large urban areas of Toronto and Montreal.

It is clear from our discussion so far that occupations are linked with regions. The Jews and Italians are heavily located in the larger urban centres where the Jews can conduct their business and the Italians can perform blue collar services in machining, construction, and processing (Reitz 1982). Because of their differential status, however, these two are fairly segregated in the cities of Toronto, Montreal, and Winnipeg, as demonstrated by Richmond (1972), Kalbach (1980), and Driedger et al. (1974). The individual needs of these two groups are rather different in that the Jews can provide for their individual and collective needs much better than the Italians, who are more dependent on government services and welfare.

Assimilation and Home Language Use

Language knowledge and use is considered by many (Lieberson 1970; Joy 1972; deVries and Vallee 1980) a highly important part of resistance to ethnic assimilation. French Canadians especially feel that if knowledge and use of their mother language wanes, assimilation is close at hand. Driedger (1975) developed ethnic identity scales using a multivariate approach to measuring ethnic identity maintenance. He included language as one of the important variables along with endogamy, religiosity, choice of friends, parochial education, and participation in ethnic organizations. Some scholars argue (Isajiw and Makabe 1982; Driedger 1975) that while language use is one of the important variables, it is not the only one to consider.

A special run of the 1981 Canada Census data of elderly persons (65 years plus) shows the extent to which the mother tongue of their ancestors was learned and the extent to which it is still used in their homes. We expected that the elderly would use their ethnic languages more than the young, because the elderly would not be as assimilated. That is, we expected language to be strongly related to generational status (immigrant, second generation, third generation, etc.). This would also provide some indication of the extent to which ethnic languages are an important part of dealing with the aged in Canada.

Table 3.4 shows that a majority of the Canadian elderly (except for the Jews) had learned the mother tongue of their ancestors when they were young, and they were still able to use it. Such knowledge was, not surprisingly, especially strong among the elderly representing the charter groups, the British (97.9 percent) and the French (92.8 percent). Most of the Chinese

TABLE 3.4

MOTHER TONGUE BY ETHNIC GROUPS AND THEIR
HOME LANGUAGE USE, AGED 65 AND OVER IN CANADA, 1981

Ethnic Origin	Mother Tongue	Home Use of Mother Tongue	Home Use of English
British	97.9%	99.0	99.0
French	92.8	88.4	11.4
African	83.3	83.3	83.3
Chinese	93.6	86.4	12.2
Dutch	53.6	23.3	70.2
German	62.3	24.7	73.8
Greek	93.2	76.3	18.6
Italian	89.6	72.4	23.1
Jewish	45.2	18.1	77.5
Polish	68.7	40.0	49.9
Portuguese	90.4	86.4	12.8
Scandinavian	57.0	5.5	94.5
Ukrainian	89.3	52.6	46.5
Other Single	60.9	42.5	49.0

SOURCE: Derived from the 2% Public Census Tape obtained from the Canadian Association on Gerontology/Association Canadienne de Gerontologie.

(93.6 percent), the Greeks (93.2 percent), the Portuguese (90.4 percent), and the Italians (89.6 percent) could use their mother tongues because a large majority are foreign-born. That is, they learned their ethnic language in their country of origin. A majority of north European elderly, such as the Dutch (53.6 percent), the Scandinavians (57.0 percent), and the Germans (62.3 percent), still know their ethnic mother tongues. Length of time in Canada is no doubt a factor. The Jews (45.2 percent) are the lowest of all.

To what extent do the current cohorts of ethnic elders still use their ethnic mother tongue? Almost all of the elderly of charter group origin use their mother tongue at home (although there is a slight decline for the French). Most African elderly either came from the United States or from former British colonies where English was their mother tongue. The Chinese and Portuguese elderly are still using their ethnic tongue at home. The Portuguese elderly came more recently and are mostly foreign-born. Many Chinese, whether they came earlier or were born here, lived largely in Chinatowns where they could maintain their language. For the Jewish elderly, and north Europeans such as the Scandinavians, Dutch, and Germans, use of their mother tongues is declining rapidly, and there are indications of language shift toward the use of English (deVries and Vallee 1980, 98, 107, 116, 122).

It is apparent, then, that knowledge and use of language varies considerably by ethnic group (deVries and Vallee 1980, 105, 113). Thus, to the extent that language use and shift (see Table 3.5) is an indicator of ethnic assimilation, assimilation varies greatly by ethnic group. It is essential for those who seek to communicate and work with the elderly to be aware of these variations and to employ people who can speak the appropriate language. Language is a highly personal part of self-identity and ethnic identity.

Religion as a Support for Ethnic Elderly

Is religion an important factor in maintenance of ethnic identity among the Canadian elderly? Table 3.6 shows that more than one-half of the Chinese elderly (54.3 percent) have no religious affiliation. However, for all others, approximately 95 percent state a religious affiliation. Most Canadian elderly do have religious affiliations, but this does not tell us which religions they are affiliated with. The religious variations among ethnic groups are interesting and the patterns vary considerably.

The French, Portuguese, Italian, and Polish elderly are almost exclusively Roman Catholic; their ethnicity and religious faith are synonymous. Since almost half of the population of Canada are Roman Catholic, the largest religious orientation consists of varied ethnic groups. The French Roman Catholics dominate the Quebec region, and the Italians and Portuguese are heavily located in larger urban centres such as Toronto and Montreal. Only the Jewish (97 percent Jewish) and the Greek elderly (94.1 percent Eastern Orthodox) conform to such an unidenominational pattern, and they too reside mostly in these larger metropolitan areas. All others are distributed into a number of religious denominations.

The British, who are the largest ethnic group in Canada, support the United Church (35.1 percent) and Anglican (25.0 percent) denominations, making them a bireligious group, with considerable numbers in the Roman Catholic (13.3 percent) and Presbyterian (10.1 percent) denominations as well. The Ukrainians have also traditionally supported two religious groups and are still well represented in the Ukrainian Catholic (37.8 percent) and Eastern Orthodox (31.5 percent) faiths, with a sizeable number having joined the Roman Catholics (11.5 percent). North European groups such as the Scandinavians, Germans, and Dutch are beginning to shift from their traditional religions to others. While one-half (51.8 percent) of the Scandinavians are still Lutheran, a sizeable number (21.5 percent) have shifted to the United Church. One-third of the Germans are still members of the Lutheran church (31.2 percent) and one-fourth are Roman Catholics (23.5 percent), but they are increasingly joining other faiths. The Dutch elderly have perhaps shifted to more denominations than any other group, although one-fourth are still Dutch Reformed. These multireligious north

TABLE 3.5

PERCENTAGE OF ETHNIC GROUP SHIFTING TO ENGLISH MOTHER TONGUE, BY AGE GROUP, CANADA, 1971

Age Group	British to French*	French	German	Italian	Dutch	Polish	Scandinavian	Ukrainian	Indian and Inuit
0–4	1.5	14.2	80.7	34.3	89.8	81.3	95.8	81.0	45.8
5–9	1.3	13.2	81.2	39.6	89.5	81.0	95.3	78.6	47.8
10–14	1.3	12.0	78.8	39.3	86.3	77.8	95.2	73.7	46.6
15–19	1.5	11.3	75.4	34.2	77.5	70.4	92.1	67.5	45.2
20–24	1.9	11.6	72.8	23.6	57.4	64.3	88.3	66.1	43.9
25–29	2.2	10.2	64.1	20.0	45.4	63.9	84.9	60.6	44.1
30–39	2.0	9.3	49.8	13.8	37.1	52.3	80.3	45.5	38.4
40–64	1.5	7.8	44.9	16.4	37.7	29.4	64.7	25.3	32.2
65 and over	1.0	6.7	39.2	10.9	46.6	15.3	36.3	8.7	24.9
Total	1.0	10.4	61.7	25.1	61.7	52.0	77.8	48.5	40.5

* Data refer to British ethnic origin shifting to French mother tongue in this case.

Source: J. deVries and F. G. Vallee, *Language Use in Canada*, p. 107 (Ottawa: Minister of Supply and Services, 1980), extracted from *Census of Population in Canada*, 1980. Reproduced with permission.

Table 3.6

Affiliation of Ethnic Elderly (Age 65 and Over) with Religious Denominations

Ethnic Origin	Roman Catholic	Ukrainian Catholic	Anglican	Baptist	Lutheran	Mennonite	Pentecostal
British	13.4%	.0	25.0	5.8	.8	.1	1.3
French	96.3	.0	.5	.4	.1	.0	.1
African	21.2		18.2	15.2	.6		10.6
Chinese	6.4		2.5	5.0	.6	.3	1.4
Dutch	15.0		7.3	4.6	1.8	12.4	2.1
German	23.5	.0	3.6	5.2	31.2	10.9	2.0
Greek	1.7		.8				
Italian	95.9		.3	.1	.2		.7
Jewish	.3		.1				.1
Polish	78.9	2.9	1.9	.4	2.5		.1
Portuguese	96.0		.8		.8		
Scandinavian	1.8		4.4	4.4	51.8		2.1
Ukrainian	11.5	37.8	1.8	1.4	.7	.2	1.1
Other Single	31.5	.6	7.1	2.1	16.5	1.1	1.0

TABLE 3.6 Continued

Ethnic Origin	Presbyterian	United Church	Other Protestant	Eastern Orthodox	Jewish	Eastern non-Christian	No Religion
British	10.1	35.1	4.8	.1	.2	.1	3.3
French	.2	1.2	.5	.0	.1	.0	.6
African	3.0	9.1	1.1	3.0		4.5	3.0
Chinese	3.4	14.1	2.8		.6	8.3	54.3
Dutch	5.0	18.6	26.2		.2		6.8
German	2.6	12.7	4.8	.1	.1	.0	3.3
Greek	.8		2.5	94.1			3.3
Italian	.4	1.2	.5	.1			.6
Jewish	.1	.1	.1		97.3		1.7
Polish	.6	3.3	1.5	2.3	2.6		2.9
Portuguese	.8	.8	.8				
Scandinavian	2.0	21.5	7.4	.1		.1	4.4
Ukrainian	.6	5.8	2.7	31.5	.3		4.8
Other Single	2.1	9.6	5.0	8.6	1.1	8.8	5.0

SOURCE: Derived from the 2% Public Census Tape obtained from the Canadian Association on Gerontology/Association Canadienne de Gerontologie.

Europeans are also very heavily concentrated in the prairies, where ethnic, political, and religious pluralism are most evident.

In sum, most of Canada's ethnic elderly belong to a religious group, and their denominational adherence varies by ethnic group. Religion is an important factor in any research on the Canadian elderly. Modernization seems, however, to influence changes from one denomination to another, which cannot be thoroughly analyzed here. Why are Scandinavians joining the United Church extensively; are Orthodox Jews shifting to the more liberal Reformed Judaism; why do Ukrainian Orthodox join the Roman Catholics? Considerable shifts are taking place. However, except for the Chinese (54.3 percent), few groups declare no religion, which we would expect if assimilation were a major factor. To examine the many religious shifts in detail requires further research.

FINDING ETH-ELDER TYPES

The discussion in Chapter 1 suggested that the ethnic elderly cluster differently demographically. The discussion here suggests the processes of modernization and assimilation also have differential affects on the many ethnic groups. Can these many variables be ordered by developing eth-elder types, located in different regions of Canada, with differential values, and needs? We propose that the aboriginal native peoples of Canada best represent a plural pre-modern type of elderly, while Jewish elders located in metropolitan areas are the best example of modernized non-assimilated types. These polar types are now expanded, and other groupings of ethnic elders are placed across this potential range. These various types probably have quite different needs and represent different problems and challenges. However, a brief discussion of regional eth-elder variations will be presented first to provide an ecological context.

Regional Variation

Table 3.7 shows almost all of the elderly in Newfoundland are of British origin (91 percent), with no other sizeable ethnic group present. The French are a large majority in Quebec, as are the British in Nova Scotia and Prince Edward Island. These regions illustrate the dominance of single ethnic groups. This means that governments in these areas can concentrate on policy that affects largely one ethnic group. However, it also means that elderly persons who are not members of these groups might be especially at risk, because they have fewer opportunities for networking with members of their own groups.

On the other hand, no ethnic group is a numerical majority in any of the three Prairie Provinces. Whereas the British are the largest group, there are also sizeable German, Ukrainian, and French elderly populations. How do

TABLE 3.7
DISTRIBUTION OF ETHNIC ELDERLY (55 YEARS PLUS) BY PROVINCE, CANADA, 1981

Ethnic Origin	Nfld.	N.S.	N.B.	P.Q.	Ont.	Man.	Sask.	Alta.	B.C.	NWT* PEI	Total Canada
British	94.3	75.8	62.6	11.3	61.0	44.4	43.5	48.3	61.8	73.1	47.5
French	2.5	9.9	31.3	76.6	6.6	6.4	4.0	4.4	3.0	11.2	24.2
African	.0	.4	.1	.2	.3	.1	.0	.1	.1	.2	.2
Chinese	.0	.0	.0	.2	.9	.4	.3	1.1	2.4	.0	.7
Dutch	.1	2.2	.6	.2	1.9	2.9	2.0	3.2	2.1	.8	1.6
German	.1	4.7	1.2	.7	5.1	10.3	17.5	11.4	7.2	.3	5.3
Greek	.0	.1	.0	.4	.4	.0	.1	.1	.2	.0	.3
Italian	.1	.3	.2	2.5	4.5	.7	.1	1.1	1.8	.2	2.6
Jewish	.1	.4	.2	2.7	2.2	2.8	.2	.6	.5	.0	1.8
Polish	.0	.4	.0	.6	2.3	4.8	2.7	2.8	1.5	.0	1.8
Portuguese	.0	.0	.0	.2	.8	.4	.2	.1	.2	.0	.4
Scandinavian	.2	.4	.5	.1	.7	3.6	6.8	6.0	4.4	.3	1.8
Ukrainian	.0	.3	.1	.5	2.5	13.8	11.2	9.7	2.8	.2	3.1
Other Single	1.1	1.6	.5	2.7	7.8	7.4	8.7	8.4	8.9	9.7	6.1
Multiple Origins	1.5	3.5	2.7	1.1	3.0	2.0	2.4	2.7	3.1	4.0	2.6
Total %	100.0	100.0	100.0	100.0	100.0	100.0	100.0	100.0	100.0	100.0	100.0

* A residual category dominated by P.E.I. numerically.

SOURCE: Derived from the 2% Public Census Tape obtained from the Canadian Association on Gerontology/Association Canadienne de Gerontologie.

prairie governments develop multiethnic policy? Should they focus on regions where one of the many groups is highly concentrated, or must they serve all equally everywhere? This multiethnic mix is also very evident in Toronto, Montreal, and Vancouver, where recent immigrants have been attracted in large numbers. Perhaps these diversities can best be served by municipal governing bodies.

There are also important ethnic islands, such as the native Indians in the Northlands, the Chinese in British Columbia, and the Jews in Toronto and Montreal. It is interesting that New Brunswick is the only area where both charter group elderly reside in large numbers, although the Ottawa-Hull urban region is now also such a bilingual-bicultural area. These ethnic variations support the need for regional variation in social policy and the necessity for local input. The fact that health care falls within provincial jurisdiction permits such variation in program design and implementation. However, it also means that setting national standards and building coherent national programs can be more difficult.

As seen in Figure 3.1, it is possible to think of at least six regions of Canada where the ethnic clustering results in differential needs of the elderly by regional types. Newfoundland, Nova Scotia, and Prince Edward Island can concentrate on the British elderly, and Quebec on the French elderly, with special attention to members of other groups who will be very much in the minority. Agencies in the West and in urban regions like Toronto must plan in multiethnic terms. The Northlands are unique because of the sparse, scattered majority of native elderly, who are disadvantaged in many respects. The elderly in New Brunswick and Ottawa must be considered in biethnic charter terms, although other groups are increasingly entering Ottawa too. With this brief ecological context we now turn to a discussion of eth-elder types.

Traditional Aboriginal Elderly

The 413,000 native people of Canada are comprised mostly of native Indians (Statistics Canada 1981). Only about 20,000 are Inuit. Native Indians come from numerous cultural areas and live in different environments. The basic homeland of these native people is the Northlands, representing about four-fifths of the Canadian land area (Figure 3.1). Native people are a majority in the Northwest Territories, which is made up of many language and cultural groups. The Inuit reside on the northern shores of the Arctic Ocean, the Hudson Bay, and the MacKenzie River delta, while native Indians are scattered throughout the Northwest Territories, the Yukon, and the northern-most parts of the six most westerly provinces (British Columbia to Quebec). While many are still located in their preindustrial aboriginal habitat, more and more are moving to settlements that

FIGURE 3.1
CULTURAL AND LINGUISTIC REGIONS, CANADA, 1981

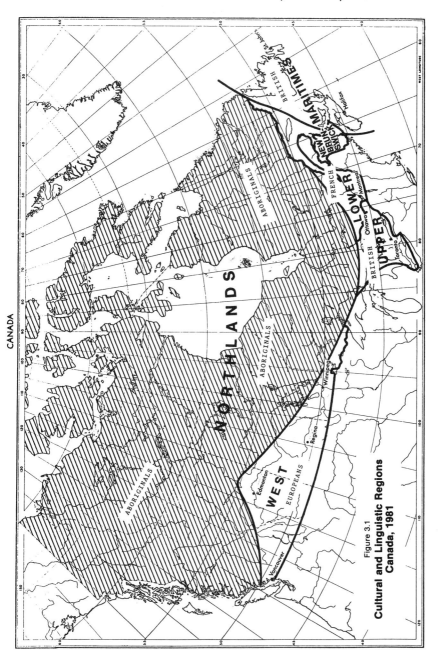

Figure 3.1
Cultural and Linguistic Regions
Canada, 1981

are increasingly influenced by mining, logging, and transport operations of non-native southern Canadians (Matthiasson and Matthiasson 1978). Many are still isolated and segregated in these vast northern spaces. Few native people have benefitted from technological and modernization changes, but native people have been extremely vulnerable to modern disadvantages.

We have also shown that a very small percentage of these traditional native peoples (3.5 percent, Table 1.1) are elderly. As with many preindustrial peoples, early deaths tend to wipe out the high birth rates, so that very few enter old age. Thus, there are only about 15,000 native people over the age of 65 in all of Canada. These elderly Indians and Inuit are still mostly located in traditional food-gathering locations up north, although more and more are locating in modern northern settlements. While it is true that large numbers of Indians are migrating to the southern cities, this is a very recent trend and most of those migrating are younger people. When these younger Indians age, there will therefore be special native elderly needs in cities.

The elderly Indian population in the United States appears to be similar to that in Canada, and they too represent only 5.3 percent of all Indians. Information is sparse in both Canada and the United States, but Edwards (1983, 75) notes the low levels of formal education among American Indians. Traditionally, Indian elderly were regarded as an important resource and held in high regard because old age was equated with wisdom and learning and respect and honour were bestowed on the elderly. They were also active in instructing the young and helping to care for children, and they "maintained responsibility for remembering and relating tribal philosophies, myths, traditions and stories" (Edwards 1983, 75-76). Fifty-one percent of American Indians over 65 years in 1980 received incomes below the poverty line, housing was very inadequate and crowded, and 55 percent of Indian women over 60 years were widowed (Edwards 1983, 76-80). In sum, the plight of the Canadian and American Indian elderly seems to be highly similar. They are a distinct, traditinal aboriginal minority living in great poverty and need.

The native elderly have not as yet entered the modernization process to a great extent. Studies (Frideres 1983; Price 1979) show that for all age groups, few have formal education beyond the elementary school level and many are still in a preliterate state. This is especially true among the elderly. Some are still engaged in hunting and fishing, many are involved in occupations such as forestry and mining, and large numbers are unemployed. Very few elderly native people have entered the technological age of work, and relatively few of the younger natives with whom they associate are industrialized. For the most part the native elderly are still in a traditional, preindustrial environment.

Because of residential segregation, the traditional native surroundings, culture, and language, most of the native people's aboriginal ethnic identity has been retained. Most of the elderly speak their native tongues, and relatively few have learned to speak, let alone read or write, either of the official Canadian languages. The Roman Catholic and Anglican religions have entered these northern parts extensively, so that many native people have adopted European Christianity, but many of the elderly either practise traditional religions or have combined their traditional version with new European forms. In this sense, the native elderly have neither assimilated nor modernized. In the future this will likely change, and more study is needed to see what future trends might bring.

Studies of the native elderly in Canada are limited, but a few American studies corroborate some of the findings in the Canadian census. Gelfand (1982, 28–30) is impressed with the persistence American Indians have demonstrated despite the ill-treatment they have received in the past. He suggests that the movements they are now starting for land claims and native rights, which he attributes to the strong oral tradition of the elderly passing on the culture to the younger generations, are an important premodern form of communication. He says Indians in the American southwest and northwest also continue to perpetuate many concepts of communal property and mutual aid, even though they were confined to reservations, a concept of private property that is foreign to them.

Block (1979, 184–85) laments the limited information on the Indian elderly, but elaborates on their "grinding poverty, substandard housing, limited education, inadequate income, poor health, malnutrition, lack of urgently needed services and their emotional problems." The problems become acute as age progresses. Reservations are increasingly left with a population consisting of the aging and the very young. The young who leave the reserve leave their elderly with no economic base except welfare grants. Tribal councils are not able to help sufficiently, because they too lack adequate funds. The former traditional family had many features of the extended family, where reverence for the elderly was common. Block (1979, 188) argues that materialism linked with economic individualism is eroding the need for the advice and experience of the elderly.

Havens (Havens and Thompson 1975) interviewed a random sample of almost 5,000 Manitobans, 65 years and older, and assessed their needs in nine categories (psychosocial, shelter, household maintenance, ethnocultural, physical health, mental health, economic, proximity to family, and availability of family). They presented their findings for seven different regions of Manitoba, comparing ten ethnic groups. This included native Canadians, so their needs could be compared with those of others. The findings show that native needs for housing were higher than any other group in all regions of Manitoba. In addition, native needs in most of the other categories were greater than those of the British, as well as most of the other ethnic groups. This is one of the few empirical studies of the native elderly in Canada. It shows in composite form that the lack of education and access to other modern conveniences leaves Manitoban aboriginals least modernized, and most in need of shelter, household maintenance, health, and other economic services.

In Winnipeg, Chappell and Strain (1984) studied a representative sample of 193 elderly (age 50 and over) native people, all permanent, long-term residents of the city. It might be expected that elderly Indians who come to the city feel alienated and alone; to what extent are they able to find social support and satisfaction in urban living? To what extent do they perpetuate their cultural identity, or does assimilation happen quickly? Table 3.8 reveals that about two-thirds (66 percent) of the native elderly in Winnipeg use their native language whenever possible. About one-fourth (22 percent) actually speak their native tongue more often than any other language, and almost one-half (46 percent) speak both their native tongue and English. Three-fourths (76 percent) report that their nearest relatives also live in Winnipeg, most are very satisfied with the relations with their family (81 percent), and almost all (95 percent) are satisfied with their relations with their family, friends, and neighbours. Most (89 percent) think church is an important centre for them, and two-thirds (61 percent) are generally satisfied with life. Three-fourths (70 percent) never or rarely feel left out of important networks, and as many never or rarely feel lonely (73 percent). Three-fourths (73 percent) feel they are treated with respect in the community.

These stable native residents (short-term residents, including seasonal residents, were not part of the study) seem not to be too adversely affected by

TABLE 3.8

ATTITUDES AND ACTIVITY OF NATIVE INDIAN ELDERLY
(50 YEARS AND OLDER) IN WINNIPEG, 1984 (N = 193)

Issues	Percent
1. Use native Indian language whenever possible	66
2. Speak the native Indian tongue most often	22
3. Speak both English and the native tongue most often	46
4. Nearest relatives live in the city	76
5. Very satisfied with relationships with their family	81
6. Satisfied with relationships with family, friends, and neighbors	95
7. Generally satisfied with life	61
8. Church is important as a spiritual center	89
9. I usually have people to talk to	60
10. I rarely or never feel left out	70
11. I rarely or never feel lonely	73
12. Indians are treated with respect in my community	73

SOURCE: Computed from N. L. Chappell and L. A. Strain, *Needs Assessment of Natives 50+ Living in Winnipeg.* (Study conducted through the Centre on Aging, University of Manitoba, 1984).

urban modern life. Is that because their resilience or adjustment is greater than expected or because their expectations and aspirations are as yet very low? We do know natives are similar to others in their responses. Most elderly non-natives, when asked, report relatively high overall well-being. This has generally been interpreted as a tendency to accept one's life, under whatever conditions, rather than expect more. But it may be that we should be devising more sensitive measures of quality of life and its various components.

Urban Jewish Elderly

We suggested earlier that the Jews in Canada represent an opposite polar type to the native peoples, in that demographically they have the largest proportion of aged (16.5 percent over 65) and are almost exclusively urban dwellers, concentrated in the largest metropolitan areas of Toronto, Montreal, and Winnipeg. They represent a sizeable minority (5–6 percent of the population) in these centres, even though in total (264,000 in 1981) they represent only 1 percent of the Canadian population. As illustrated earlier, Canada's Jews are also most highly educated and they are most heavily represented in the sales, managerial, literary, and health occupations, which makes them the highest occupational status group in Canada. Numerically, the Jews are smaller than Canada's native people, but they are influential beyond their numbers in the modern economic and political spheres.

Even though the Jewish elderly in Canada have urbanized and modernized, they have not assimilated. They are heavily residentially segregated in urban areas (Driedger and Church 1974; Kalbach 1980), and they have centred their ethnic identity around a distinctive religion among the overwhelming Canadian Christian majority. Although Jews have been quick to adopt languages as needed, studies (Driedger 1980; Weinfeld et al. 1981) show that they intermarry less, adhere to their distinctive religion and frequent Jewish institutions more, than most other ethnic groups. They have maintained their identity and have not been assimilated in the modern, industrial Canadian setting.

Studies of the Jewish elderly are limited, but some important contributions do exist (Guttmann 1973; A. Rose 1981). Of relevance here are those studies pointing to the diversity among this group. In the United States, Kaplan (1979) found that programs that attracted older Jewish adults born in Eastern Europe were unable to meet the needs of the better educated, American-born Jewish aged. The American-born were more purposeful in their leisure patterns, while the Eastern foreign-born were more group-oriented in their activities. Guttmann (1973, 220–23) pursued these findings in a study of a Jewish community centre in Baltimore and found that the foreign-born who came out of East European Shtetls emphasized orthodox education and a greater knowledge of Hebrew than the native-born. Both groups used both Yiddish and English. All American-born elderly had elementary education, compared to only half of those born in Eastern Europe. Seventy percent of the Americans had a high school education, and 30 percent were college or university graduates; none of the foreign-born had college education, and only 45 percent had high school diplomas.

Those born in Eastern Europe were more interested in group activities, while elderly born in America preferred artistic activities like painting, sculpture, entertainment, sports (golf and baseball), and more individualistic forms of expression. However, both groups were interested in entertainment and in celebrating Jewish holidays. This study shows that even within ethnic groups the elderly have very different needs, depending on socialization, education, and orientation, and this has important implications for service needs. The American-born Jewish elderly were more oriented than those born in Eastern Europe toward modern activities, although they were not necessarily more assimilated.

A. Rose (1981, 193-204) reviewed a number of Canadian studies that throw further light on "myths" of Jewish family responsibility, the self-sufficiency of Jewish elderly, and the extent of the response of the Jewish community to their elderly in Canada. Rose argues that modern life has significantly weakened the extended family, and that mobility has been an important part of the family scattering, leaving the elderly in cities more alone than previously. Many of their children and grandchildren are now far away. However, with respect to self-sufficiency, Rose reviewed studies in Toronto and Vancouver that showed the Jewish elderly were relatively well housed and adequately provided with income and that very few were destitute. He found that in the psychosocial, food and clothing, physical health, mental health, and accessibility to resources categories, needs exceeded resources, although there were few severe cases.

> Within Toronto's huge Jewish population, some 17,000 perhaps or 15% are over sixty; nearly half of this group are described as "camp survivors," with a complex of psychological factors complicating the normal emotional and economic aspects of aging. The head of the Jewish Family and Child Service claimed in late 1978 that almost one in every four Jewish elderly was "at risk." [A. Rose 1981, 199-200]

This clearly illustrates how special historical events create needs, even for communities that generally provide for their aged. The Toronto Jewish community created the Baycrest Geriatric Centre to deal with some of these needs. This is a good example of how it is possible to focus on a specific need when the elderly are located in one city where the ethnic community can support their elderly. Other Jewish homes for the elderly can be found in Montreal, Toronto, Winnipeg, and Vancouver as an outgrowth of early immigrant needs, so that Jews in need could find help "among their own." When the elderly of a group such as the Jews are located in a few urban centres, where the population mass is sufficient to create facilities, it is much easier to help than with such elderly as those of Canada's aboriginal peoples who are scattered in northern areas where population density is very sparse. In this sense the Jews utilize modern forms of providing for their elderly, while at the same time using their ethnic group as a resource for meeting needs.

European Prairie Farm Elders

Having presented the two polar types — the rural aboriginal and the urban Jewish elderly — other ethnic groups can now be placed within this range. Many of the ethnic elderly in the prairie West represent elements of both types presented so far, and when new combinations are created, a third type emerges. Again social context, needs, and aspirations may be different, so that ethnic conditions must be taken into account.

In the discussion of demographic regions, it was illustrated that elderly people of British, German, Ukrainian, French, Scandinavian, and Dutch European origin are prominent in the Prairie Provinces, where there is a multicultural and multilingual setting of agriculturalists. These elderly farmers of European origin represent the pioneers who opened up the West to agriculture, a way of life quite different from aboriginal food-gathering in the Northlands, or the urban Jewish managerial, sales, and literary enterprise. These prairie elderly found themselves in vast open spaces similar to those inhabited by the Indians, but they settled down on farms, with access to village and town centres from which they got their supplies and which acted as a community centre for their social and church needs. Many of these prairie elderly of European origin now live in these small villages, hamlets, and towns, which provide some focus for services and protect them from isolation.

A. B. Anderson (1972) studied nine ethnic bloc settlements in the region surrounding Saskatoon and found that many of the inhabitants perpetuated their ethnic ways of life. Each of these ethnic groups lived in fairly distinct, segregated rural farm areas. The Hutterites are perhaps the best example of exclusive ethnic enclaves, but they also form cultural islands and have sustained their unique origins for a long time. Endogamy and church attendance were very high, and their ability to speak their mother tongues and frequent use of their language were also high. These rural ethnic enclaves provide stable security with limited mobility for the elderly, who can move to nearby hamlets and villages. Many ethnic churches have been moved to town, where businesses are often run by entrepreneurs who speak their language. Some towns are known for their clusters of elderly people who often socialize together.

The prairie elderly's children, who continue to farm in the community, are nearby when needed. Like the aboriginals and Jews, family ties are believed to be strong and kin to be easily accessible. Like Indians on reserves, or Jews in segregated urban areas, these European elderly are clustered in communities. Most of these elderly are better off economically than native elderly however, and like the Jews, their needs can be met more easily in small towns, although their demographic mass is not as great for support of institutions. These prairie elderly have not modernized as much as the Jews occupationally; however their small-town lifestyle is more leisurely, and movement is not as restricted as it is for the Jews in the city. They can read and write, although their literary and artistic interests have not been extensively developed. These elderly are not assimilated. Although their introduction to the modern society has begun, it has not escalated.

Havens and Thompson (1975) studied the British, Germans, Ukrainians, French, Scandinavians, and Poles in the agricultural heartland of prairie Manitoba. Here the British dominated in the Westman region, the Ukrainians in the Parkland region, the French in Eastman Region, and the Dutch and Germans in south central Manitoba. There was little difference between the needs of these elderly with respect to psychosocial, shelter, household maintenance, ethno-cultural, physical health, mental health, economic, proximity to family, and availability of resource factors in any of the regions.

Needs of the native Indians were distinctive, but those of the other groups were not. This suggests, as we would expect, that these European prairie elderly have roughly the same occupational, family, religious, institutional, and economic support that can be provided in rural small towns, even if the elderly of each of these groups like to be among people of their own ethnic group. Except for the Protestant-Catholic differentiation, many of these elderly prairie ethnics appear to accept others when they enter church-related public homes for the elderly. Prairie villages and hamlets seem to be ideal places to retire in, where contact with kin, friends, and neighbours remains roughly intact. Research specific to this area is required, but it can be suggested that it represents a form of modified identity and modernization.

Elderly of the French Charter Minority

There are differences between the French elderly in Quebec, part of an 80 percent French majority, and those in other parts of Canada, where they are a minority. On the prairies, the elderly in French rural communities are similar to other Europeans, representing one of many ethnic communities. In a similar way, there are important French communities in Nova Scotia, in an environment where the British dominate. In New Brunswick there is the unique situation of an officially bilingual and bicultural province, where the two official groups, the British and French, seek to run the province. However, since most of the French in New Brunswick live in the northern part of the province, hugging the Quebec border, they are also in many ways an extension of Quebec, as Joy suggested in his theory of the bilingual belt (1972). The focus here shall be on the French elderly in Quebec, who are unique in Canada.

Perhaps more than anywhere else, there is within one province an enormous process of modernization and counter-assimilation in Quebec. The French, the junior partner in the charter agreement, are pursuing the Quiet Revolution, moving from almost feudal forms of rural life to urbanization at a tremendous pace, politically, economically, and socially (Rioux 1971). Thus, within one region there are very different needs among the French elderly. How are these elderly coping with the rush to modernization and urbanization? We expect that there are French rural prairie elderly types, as well as many Jewish types. A revolution of values, norms, and beliefs among the French aged is also in process. How does this affect their security and well-being?

In the earlier discussion of the demographics of the ethnic elderly, French birth rates were shown to be high until recently, resulting in a smaller proportion of elderly (7.8 percent) than the national average. Almost all of these elderly are Canadian-born (99.4 percent), and the vast majority live in the region of Quebec where the French dominate. While these French elderly represent 23.2 percent of all Canadians 55 years and older, they represent 37.7 percent of all elderly with grade five or less and only 16.2 percent of all elderly with a bachelor's degree. The French are a large majority (89.4 percent) of all elderly in Quebec City, they are also a majority (58.7 percent) in Montreal, and represent one-third (30.8 percent) of the elderly in Ottawa-Hull. Most of them are retired from occupations overrepresented in lower primary (31.4 percent) and processing (30.9 percent) work. More than any group, they have strongly retained their identity. Of the French elderly (65 years plus), 92.8 percent can still use their mother tongue, and 88.4 percent use it at home. Ninety-six percent are Roman Catholic; almost all (99.4 percent) belong to a religious group. The French elderly in Canada are modernizing while at the same time maintaining a strong French identity.

The French were the first of the Europeans to settle in Canada more than 350 years ago along the St. Lawrence River, where they set up their seigniorial villages and the narrow strip rang land plan. Miner (1939) illustrates well folk village life in the 1930s in a Quebec rural village with its kinship patterns, the important role of the Roman Catholic religion, social organization of village life, and its traditional ways. However, even in the 1930s Miner wrote about changes taking place, so that St. Denis was beginning to lose its folk character. Most of the French elderly grew up in such rural folk environments. They have also seen the effects of industrialization described by Hughes (1943) in his study of Cantonville, where he illustrates increased stratification of French workers in lower status jobs. Rioux and Martin (1964) provide us with a description of the sweep of modernization that is taking place in Quebec, often referred to as the Quiet Revolution.

More than any other group of elderly (native elderly excluded perhaps), the aged in Quebec have seen the crisis of modernization take place, described well by Rioux (1971). Rioux traces the process of change from

Frenchmen to rural habitants, to defeat and dominance by the English, where they groomed the quiet conservatism of a colonized people. The "springtime of Quebec" and the separatist movement are both part of a modernizing Quebec, with the French becoming ever stronger to fight their "national" cause. This enormous change from habitants to modern urban dwellers took place during the lifetime of most French elderly in Quebec. Many now live in modernized rural villages, such as St. Pascal described by Gold (1975). Others have moved to the urban centres.

These French Canadians of habitant background resemble many elderly persons of the western prairies in that they were agriculturalists who loved the land. French Canadians, however, have been in Canada three to four times as long as the prairie elderly, their communities were much more stable, and as one of the founding charter groups, they have received guarantees that their language and culture will be perpetuated. Both of these traditional agricultural types can be placed somewhere between the aboriginal food gatherers and the urban Jews. We suggest the French in Quebec have become more modernized than many native peoples, but not yet as urbanized as the Jews. Many elderly of all four types have not assimilated, but represent different variations of the ethnic mosaic.

Myth of the British Majority Type

Assimilation theory implies that all ethnic groups are moving toward the British majority, making a more homogeneous society, and that this is desirable. Modernization theory assumes that change is taking place toward more modern forms and that this results in a decline in the status of the aged. So far our discussion of ethnic elderly types illustrates that changes toward assimilation and modernization are more complex and more multidimensional than these theories suggest. This section addresses both the truth and the myth about the British majority type, because the British are neither a majority nor a homogeneous group. Often they are not the most modern ethnic group, and the English, Scots, Irish, and Welsh are also influenced by processes of change.

The British are the largest charter group in Canada, representing 40.2 percent of the population. A hundred years ago, the British were indeed a majority, but no ethnic group in Canada is now a majority. The British elderly over 65 years of age do represent almost half (49.3 percent) of the elderly in Canada (Statistics Canada 1981). However, this will decline steadily because only 39.3 percent of all Canadians under 65 are of British origin (Table 1.1). Over half of all elderly persons with bachelor's degrees are British (56.2 percent); they are disproportionately represented in the higher status occupations; their English language is dominant; and they belong to the higher status Anglican and United Church religious denominations. Large numbers of these elderly are located in industrial urban southern Ontario, the original heartland of the Empire Loyalists. This is the modern industrial magnet, where British elderly of higher status and economic and political power are located, and to which many across Canada are attracted.

The problem with the Anglo-conformity model is that it assumes that the British are a homogeneous group. It can be illustrated, however, that they are heterogeneous, which supports a counterargument to the Anglo-conformity myth. One-fourth of these British elderly are foreign-born, one-third (35 percent) of all foreign-born Canadian elderly are of British origin, so immigrants do not belong only to smaller minorities. However, it is doubtful that this factor is as important for British elderly as it is for Ukrainians, for example. Significant numbers of British elderly are represented in all regions of Canada, and the different lifestyles in these various social contexts have already been mentioned. There are British miners and foresters in the Northlands, agriculturalists on the prairies, industrialists in upper Canada, minority Anglo-Saxons in Quebec, and a British majority in the Atlantic provinces, especially Newfoundland. The British majority of elderly in Newfoundland and the British minority in Quebec are excellent examples of the diversity of British elderly in Canada (i.e., the British are a diverse group even internally).

The British dominate in Newfoundland as they do in no other part of Canada. Newfoundland is the poorest province in Canada, where unemployment is high; in that sense the situation of many Newfoundlanders is similar to that of many native Indians of the Northlands. Newfoundland is one of the least urbanized regions in Canada, where large numbers of elderly were engaged in the fishing industry, a lower occupational and income group. The province is very British still, because Newfoundland joined the dominion only recently, and it is isolated in eastern Canada, where it has been hard to attract industry. Although modernization is slowly progressing, many elderly still find themselves isolated in fishing villages, far from modern conveniences. The elderly do not have much education, their incomes are low, and modern technology has not been greatly developed. These British elderly are very different from their urban, industrial, upper Canadian cousins.

Another distinctly different British group is the minority that resides in dominantly French Quebec. The British elderly (10.8 percent) are a relatively small minority, although their control of parts of the Quebec economy is still considerable (Hughes 1943; Rioux 1971). Nevertheless, like all minorities in Canada, they struggle for their survival in the educational system and have relatively little influence in Quebec politics. Many older Anglo-Saxons are moving out of the dominantly francophone Quebec to Ontario, to retire in an anglophone environment. It is interesting that British minority elders are as concerned with assimilation and powerlessness in Montreal as are many other minority elders elsewhere in Canada. Their problems seem to be highly similar.

We propose that the elderly of British origin in southern Ontario, in Newfoundland, and in southwestern Quebec live in very different social environments. They often have different needs, and power to change their circumstances varies considerably. Adding these three British groups to British prairie farmers and primary workers in the north raises the interesting question whether the British in Canada are as distinctive a dominant ethnic type as assimilationists and Anglo-conformity theorists suggest. It is hard to decide. We propose that they are too diverse internally to be a distinctive type like the Indians, Jews, north European agriculturalists, or French Québécois (granted there are variations here too). In this sense a dominant British majority elderly type is a myth.

SUMMARY

In this chapter we have sought to gather some empirical evidence to frame the macro-trends of the ethnic elderly in Canada. This helped to link empirical evidence with the modernization and assimilation themes that were developed in Chapter 2. It is evident, however, that modernization and assimilation processes are multidimensional, complex, and not necessarily related to one another.

By means of a descriptive demographic history, Chapter 1 touched on four crucial factors: the link between ethnicity and the elderly, the first-generation foreign-born population, gender differentials, and the distribution of ethnic elders in different regions of Canada. The Jews have a very large elderly population compared to the native peoples, and other groups also vary considerably. There are almost no foreign-born French Canadians in Canada. Two-thirds of the foreign-born elderly belong to non-charter groups, because of the recent flow of immigrants to Canada. While most elderly men are married, half of the elderly women are widowed, so that elderly women are faced with different kinds of social problems than most elderly men. The distribution of these ethnic elderly also varies enormously by region, with the native elderly scattered in the Northlands, farm elderly often moving to small towns in the West, Jewish elderly concentrated in metropolitan areas, the French concentrated along the St. Lawrence in Quebec, and the British isolated in coastal villages in the Maritimes. All of these factors make for a very diverse elderly population in Canada.

In our search for evidence of modernization and assimilation among the elderly, vast differences were found among the many ethnic groups. The educational level of Jewish and British elderly is much higher than Indian and Portuguese aged. The Jews, Chinese, and Italians almost all live in metropolitan centres like Toronto and Montreal, while the native peoples are more rural. The Jewish and British elderly are overrepresented in higher level managerial and business occupations, while the aboriginal people, Portuguese, and Italians are more likely to be found in lower status jobs.

These three indicators of modernization show that the range of modernization among ethnic elderly is enormous, so that some ordering of types is necessary in order to make a degree of analytical sense.

While the indicators of assimilation or ethnic identity are limited, language and religion do provide some information. For example, ability to speak the mother tongue and home use of the mother tongue vary enormously. Many north Europeans who have been here for several generations are shifting to English, while more recent immigrants such as the Italians, Greeks, and Portuguese use their mother tongues extensively. The French and Chinese elderly also maintain their language extensively. Religion is also an important source of ethnic support. French, Italian, and Portuguese elderly are almost all Roman Catholic, while north Europeans are found within various groups of Protestants. Ethnicity and religion no doubt correlate strongly among some elderly, but not among others. Except for the Chinese, practically all of the elderly belong to a religious group. These two indicators suggest that language and religion are important factors that differentiate ethnic elders in Canada.

The need to develop some order out of the enormous ethnic variations is quite apparent (Driedger 1985). By combining socioeconomic status, geographic residence, and identity, different clusters of ethnic types emerged. We proposed two polar ethnic elderly types, the native peoples and the Jews, with the others located in between these two polar types. As a result, four eth-elder types were discussed, and the widespread belief in a dominant British type was questioned because of the internal diversity of the British (see Figure 3.2).

The traditional aboriginal elderly scattered in the vast Northlands of Canada are the closest to the food-gathering stage and have the lowest education, income, and occupational status. They are the poorest, and also the most needy economically. However, they seem to be well integrated into their families and communities, so that social alienation and loss of status may not be as severe as it would otherwise be. Some traditional prestige may linger, and the aboriginal elderly may have less status loss than many

FIGURE 3.2

**EMERGING ETH-ELDER TYPES PLOTTED ON A
TRADITIONAL-MODERN CONTINUUM**

more modernized others. Research is required to examine these issues further.

In many ways, European agricultural elders who are retired on farms and in small towns on the prairies may also have retained some continuity with their past by modernizing slowly and staying within the context of their family and community. These prairie elders are also much better off economically than aboriginals or recent immigrants, so they are proposed as a distinctive type. The French elderly along the St. Lawrence in rural villages in dominantly French Quebec resemble these prairie elderly, coming from an agricultural rural base. However, they live in a more ethnically homogeneous hinterland, and they have more political power to maintain their charter language and culture. While change on the prairies came gradually, the Quiet Revolution in Quebec has brought about modernization at an enormous pace, probably affecting French elderly in the towns and cities more than in the rural villages. The European elderly on the prairies and the French elderly Quebecers are distinctive ethnic rural hinterland types.

Jewish elderly, located in the largest centres, Toronto and Montreal, are well off economically and they are more educated and have modernized more than any other group. While they often remain in segregated urban enclaves where family, community, and institutions are close at hand, they have much to lose in terms of status by abrupt retirement from their work. However, their close family and religious ties seem to a large extent to have sustained them. Assimilation has been resisted even though modernization has made great inroads.

The British elderly must be treated separately, because as the largest ethnic and charter group in Canada, they are often thought of as a special dominant type of their own. Although a case could be made for a special type on the basis of size and political and economic power, they tend to represent each of the last three types described above, depending on where in Canada we look. They are like the Jewish, modernized high status type in southern Ontario, they are more like the uniethnic demographic type of the French in Newfoundland, and they can also be found in great numbers on the prairies and in rural Ontario as prairie agricultural types. Their political and economic dominance seems unique. However, ethnically they do not cluster well into one ethnic type. The existence of a dominant British ethnic type seems to be a myth.

Having reviewed the demographic history, the various social changes taking place, and the development of specific ethnic elderly types in Canada, their needs and resources are addressed in more detail later. This chapter has provided the macro-social context for an examination of the more micro or individual needs and resources of the ethnic elderly. The next chapter examines the relevance of status and identity within the context of the treatment of older members of the group. To do so, we turn to the micro level of small group relations.

CHAPTER 4

SOCIAL STATUS AND ETH-ELDER ROLES

Some of the major theoretical perspectives in gerontology, in ethnicity, and in the small but growing area of ethnic aging were reviewed in Chapter 2. Modernization theory argues that elderly people lose status in contemporary society, compared with the past. Ethnic assimilationists argue that over time there is a loss of ethnic identity, which presumably continues into old age. Several basic questions emerge. Do the elderly lose status and to what extent does this vary by ethnicity? Are various ethnic groups assimilating or retaining their identity and how does this affect life during old age? As modernization increases, which aspects of ethnic assimilation follow and under what circumstances? If the elderly maintain high ethnic identity, what relevance does this have for their status?

So far, the discussion suggests that the degrees and types of assimilation vary from one ethnic group to another. Furthermore, social and economic mobility and therefore high social status, in the sense used in modernization theory, is not necessarily associated with assimilation, that is, with a loss of ethnic identity. A prime example here are the Jews. The Jews have achieved high status while maintaining high ethnic identity. The Germans and Chinese also rank relatively high in terms of three standard indicators of socioeconomic status — occupation, income, and education.

One reason for concern over the status and retention of ethnic identity among old people involves their place within primary-group relations. For example, in societies where old people are accorded high status, it is believed they receive more respect and better living conditions than in societies where they have low status. Similarly, ethnic groups are frequently characterized by respect for their elderly members, familism, cohesion, and so forth. The importance of primary social patterns and groups was implicit in Chapter 3. It looks as though the aboriginal elderly are well integrated into their families and communities, even though they have low educational, income, and occupational status. Similarly, European agricultural elders retired on farms in small towns in the prairies may be well integrated into their respective families and communities.

Further, the explanation for those groups who attain high status within the society but also maintain ethnic identity may well be found in primary-group relations. Ethnic culture is a source of ethnic identity and a major determinant of behaviour. It is within our primary-group relations that we interpret the world around us. The importance of this subjective level has been recognized in suggested revisions to the modernization theory in aging. Rhoads (1984), for example, argues that the value system may be the crucial intervening variable or conditioning factor in the process and outcome of modernization and in determining the position of the aged in society. Rhoads's study of Samoans supports this view.

In a similar manner, Osako's (1979) study of Japanese Americans indicates that the emphasis on group goal orientation and acceptance of dependence are foremost in how the Issei cope with their children's upward mobility. Krickus (1980) studied family relations among East Europeans and notes that commitment is deeply imbedded in family centredness rather than in individual needs. This author argues for the centrality of the family, which is seen in the reluctance to seek outside help and the difficulties in adjustment when having to move away from home to places such as nursing homes.

Recognition of the importance of the social-psychological level is evident in Canadian research as well. Thomas and Wister (1984) argue that differences in living arrangements among ethnic groups reflect variations in normative beliefs and practices concerning specific living arrangements. They postulate that differences between the British and French may be due to the tighter network of kin relations among the French, leading to higher rates of co-residence. The British, however, appear to adhere to norms of privacy and independence. They also argue that the Jewish culture promotes independent living to an even greater degree than the British by stressing educational attainment and upward mobility. These authors find ethnicity has a greater effect on living arrangements than income or financial resources.

Further, we know that cultural and ethnic factors can enter into the evaluation of social status. Burshtyn and Smith (1978, 249–73) asked northern high school students of Métis, Indian, Inuit, and European origin to rate occupational prestige. The results were then compared with a sample of national Canadians. Skilled trades such as a diesel mechanic, bulldozer operator, skidoo repairman, airplane mechanic, road building crew, and truck driver appeared as the first factor for northern students, presumably because such outdoor skills are important means of survival. On the other hand, another factor, labelled moral tone, was associated with occupations that related to the use of alcohol and the like, also an important part of northern life. Burshtyn and Smith (1978, 254–55) also found important differences between the two groups. Northern students valued radio operators, office workers, and clerks in stores highly, while national Canadian students valued physicians, scientists, lawyers, and clergymen much more. This study indicates the importance of the social context for evaluation of occupational prestige.

The extent to which factors related to modernization and socioeconomic status are important to the elderly in evaluating prestige, especially after they are retired, is not known; nor is the extent to which this varies by ethnicity known. It is doubtful that Hutterite elders worry much about their status in the larger society; whether they are valued within the colony (and evidence suggest they are, Hostetler and Huntington 1967) is more important to them. Much more research is required to learn the extent to which eth-elders desire status within their immediate peer and ethnic group and the extent to which status in the larger society is important to them. Part of this research should include a study of the boundaries of the individual's world, without assuming the larger society is transported to the local level in a simple, straightforward manner. Prestige assigned to an individual can vary depending on whether it is prestige in the neighbourhood, in the local community, nationally, among friends, among colleagues, and so forth. We do not know under what circumstances economic standing in the community is a major determinant of prestige, or when health or interpersonal power is the major determinant.

There is a dearth of literature available on the importance of ethnic culture during old age, the importance of ethnic culture for maintaining ethnic identity during this latter stage of our lives, and the relevance of ethnic culture for status, especially in Canada.

There is also another reason for concern over the role of the elderly and their place within primary-group relations. That reason relates to the support and assistance the elderly receive from the primary group, from family and friends. This area is directly relevant to policy makers and practitioners, because informal support from family and friends frequently affects the need for formal care services. There is a considerable amount of literature available (much of it from the United States) on the relevance of ethnic culture for care and assistance during old age. This no doubt has arisen from concern among gerontologists about the provision of care as health begins to deteriorate. The remainder of this chapter focuses on the issue of support for elderly members who belong to ethnic groups.

SUPPORT FOR ETH-ELDERS

Belief in the supportiveness of informal relations for members of ethnic groups is easy to find in the literature. Manuel (1982), for example, notes the minority elderly have often adopted distinguishable strategies for successfully coping with their problems. An advantage is the supportive nature of the informal network. Mindel and Wright (1982) argue that with respect to American blacks, the extended family has been a vital and vigorous system necessary for survival in an environment that is hostile and restrictive in permitting access to more formal, institutional sources of support. Informal support acts as an alternative system. The belief in the supportiveness of the informal networks of ethnic groups is common throughout the literature and seems to be applied to most groups, not only blacks (Colen and McNeely 1983, 21). For example, Lum (1983) discusses informal support among elderly Asian Americans, John (1985) in relation to elderly native Americans, and Markides et al. (1986) in relation to elderly Mexican Americans.

Less common is the view expressed by Gelfand (1982, 48) that whether the family meets the intimate confidant needs of ethnic aged people varies by cultural orientation and resources, as well as by the demand placed on all the generations in the ethnic family. Support for this alternative view is evident, for example, in the work of Grebler et al. (1970, reported in Martinez 1979), where living arrangements, visiting patterns, and relations with the extended kin group among Mexican Americans were found to decline in importance with increased urbanization, acculturation, and contact with the dominant system.

Like so much research, most of the literature in this area is American rather than Canadian. As such, much of it centres on blacks and on Mexican Americans, two groups that are less numerous in Canada, but like Canadian Indians are at the lower end of the socioeconomic scale. Further, the American literature frequently compares blacks or Mexican Americans with whites or "Anglos." Their category of whites or Anglos is problematic because it frequently refers to a combination of several categories. As Rosenthal (1983) indicates, this category is more precisely *Caucasian*, a term referring to race and not ethnicity. The term *Anglo* can refer to a racial category, a language group, or the ideal type of modern family. When this group is used in ethnic studies, however, it tends to group all individuals of European extraction together. It can include any mix of Canadians, Americans, British, and north and west Europeans.

Ethnic studies in Canada frequently distinguish ancestral origins even within the British Isles, perhaps because of their greater prominence here. As already noted, an overwhelming proportion of the Canadian population is "white." Rosenthal goes on to note that in the Canadian context the term *Anglo* as a synonym for *white* is especially misleading because many of our social concerns relate not to conflicts between blacks and whites, but between English and French. In Quebec, *Anglo* may mean any English-speaking person regardless of ethnic origin. As already pointed out (see Chapter 3), the large percentage of the Canadian population who have British ancestry suggests *Anglo* can refer to a particular ethnic group. However, as noted in the earlier discussion, even those British ancestry can differ tremendously from one another.

In addition to the relatively few studies on the ethnic elderly in Canada, many of those that do exist focus on a single group, making comparisons difficult (Guemple 1980; Tilquin et al. 1980; Chan 1983). Studies also tend to focus on different concepts and variables, adding to problems of comparison. Finally, since most research is cross-sectional, drawing conclusions over time from one generation to the next is difficult.

American Ethnic Elderly and Support Patterns

Even the American literature is inconclusive when it comes to the question whether specific ethnic groups have the advantage of an extended family and a more extended informal network. Not knowing what constitutes the white group makes extrapolation difficult; nevertheless existing data are suggestive of important ethnic differences. For example, research reported by Blau et al. (1979) suggests ethnicity exerts more powerful effects than age on health and disability, on activities, social supports, self-concept, well-being, and on economic dependency and the need for public services. Comparing Mexican Americans, blacks, and whites, these authors argue that the race-ethnicity factor constitutes "the most fundamental division in American society at the present time." Many of the ethnic differences persist when socioeconomic status is controlled.

Studying the white, black, and Spanish elderly in inner New York City, Cantor (1979) reports that the Spanish-speaking elderly most likely have children with whom they have ongoing contact, even when controlling for other factors. Mindel and Wright (1982) report major racial differences in patterns of utilization of social services between blacks and whites due to the more important role of the informal family support system for the black elderly. These authors note that for blacks, formal and informal sources of aid combine to provide important resources for the very needy. They report, however, that for whites, the extended family network is minimal or absent. In a select group of Hispanic and white elderly in a case management system, Greene and Monahan (1984) report that elderly Hispanic clients are more functionally impaired in activities of daily living than their white counterparts, but consume lower levels of agency community services. The mediating factor is a reliance on informal sources of support.

Among studies of other ethnic groups, some support for the hypothesis of greater social integration among those with ethnic or minority group ties can also be found. Krickus (1980) notes that east European women still have a strong sense of ethnic identity and commitment to the family. Krickus did not compare them with other women explicitly, but the implicit assumption is that they have a greater commitment to the family than other whites. Adams (1980) states that most minority elderly in San Diego county seek out family members or rely on them for assistance. Nevertheless, variations were found between ethnic groups. The Japanese American elderly varied more in their preference for assistance. The majority would seek out family members for transportation or small amounts of money and physical help around the house. The Latino elderly were more likely to go to family members for all service needs. The black elderly used friends and neighbours more frequently than the other two groups. Cohler (1979) argues that closeness across generations is particularly characteristic of families who came from traditional peasant societies in eastern and southern Europe.

Contrary to the above, other studies show that members of ethnic groups do not differ from one another and do not differ from "whites." When Adams (1980) controlled for age, family member living status, income, and education, the ethnic differences discussed above between Japanese, Latino, and black elderly largely disappeared. Cantor's study of whites, blacks, and Spanish in inner New York City (1979) found that the elderly who are younger, male, of higher social class, and with greater functional ability are more likely than others to live with their spouse, regardless of race or ethnicity. The higher the income, the greater the likelihood of having a functional sibling and the greater the frequency of contacts with brothers or sisters. Cantor argues that the underlying determinant of support from kin is socioeconomic status and health. As she points out, however, neither the black nor white elderly have been foresaken by their children.

It is interesting that family ties that may mitigate strain are also sources of conflict. Although stresses associated with interaction are understudied, Cohler (1979) reports frequent strain within working class families, such as the Italians and the Poles. Here, much of the day-to-day contact and exchange of resources is maintained by women, who generally serve as family kin keepers. Cohler and Grunenbaum (1981) found feelings of resentment among Italian American families regarding burdensome obligations, including demands for assistance and support from close relatives. These authors suggest that this resentment is a result of developmental personality changes at midlife; the realization that there is less time in life than before.

Wolf et al. (1983) demonstrate that distance from an older person's household is the strongest determinant of frequency of contact with family and friends for black elders, as shown previously in studies of white elders. For working class elders, whether black or white, the neighbourhood seems to be the locus of most socializing. Hanson et al. (1983) studied filial responsibility and obligations of adult children to meet the needs of their aging parents, especially in the post-retirement years. They found that, in general, filial responsibility was not supported among either blacks or whites.

Mitchell and Register (1984) found limited support for the argument that elderly blacks are more likely to receive support from family than are whites. The blacks in their study were more likely than whites to receive help from their children and grandchildren, even when controlling for socioeconomic status. They were also more likely than whites to take grandchildren, nieces, and nephews into their homes to live, regardless of socio-economic status or whether the respondent lived in a rural or urban area. Elderly whites, however, considering all categories of visitation, saw their children and grandchildren more frequently than blacks did. Although the differences were statistically significant, they were small, and the authors argued that socioeconomic status appears more influential than race when explaining whether elderly people give help to their children or grandchildren. Those without resources tend to share what they have with their children and grandchildren. The authors suggest need for help may be a primary determinant of providing assistance.

Data from the United States support the notion that generalization from findings for one ethnic group to ethnic groups in general is hazardous. Further, current knowledge does not permit firm conclusions regarding the relative importance or nature of interaction between ethnicity, health, and social class. However, there are data to suggest that some groups are characterized by the types of informal group interaction attributed to ethnic groups.

INFORMAL NETWORKS OF CANADIAN ETHNIC ELDERS

Fewer studies are available on Canada's ethnic groups and their informal networks. Nevertheless, there is some research underway. Much data do not support the notion of greater extended networks among the ethnic elderly. Single group studies suggest similarities with the elderly in general. Studying the aged in Quebec, Tilquin et al. (1980) report that absence of a spouse or children is a high-risk factor for contact with the institutional network. This is consistent with findings reported for other elderly (Shanas 1979). Both Sugiman and Nishio's (1983) study of elderly Japanese Canadians and Chan's (1983) study of elderly Chinese Canadian women indicate that they prefer not to live with their children or depend on their support. This is similar to findings reported for several industrialized countries (Myers 1982), which show that increasing proportions of elderly persons choose to live alone. The trend is consistent with the concept of intimacy-at-a-distance (Rosenmayr and Kockeis 1963), preferred by so many elderly. They wish to maintain their autonomy while interacting frequently with their children.

Other studies, explicitly comparing groups, support the notion of ethnic differentiation. Wong and Reker (1985) studied coping strategies among the Anglo and Chinese elderly and report that the Chinese elderly are more likely to depend on family members than others. As noted earlier in this chapter, Thomas and Wister (1984) report differences in living arrangements by ethnicity. Strain and Chappell (1984) find differences among elderly native and non-native residents of Winnipeg. Native people are more likely to live with someone else, to live with more than one other person, to live with someone other than a spouse, and to live with children and grandchildren. Native Indians also report more relatives outside of the household, more children, more grandchildren, more siblings, more other relatives, and more friends. That is, aboriginals have more people available

TABLE 4.1a

ETHNICITY BY MARITAL STATUS
AGED 65 AND OVER, CANADA, 1981

(A) Marital Status

Ethnic Group	Single	Married	Divorced/ Separated	Widowed	N
British	7.9%	56.4%	3.4%	32.3%	21,638
French	11.9	54.5	3.2	30.4	9,997
British & French	10.2	48.0	5.1	36.7	373
British & Other	8.7	54.1	4.2	33.1	529
French & Other	11.1	45.7	4.9	38.3	81
Chinese	2.2	41.0	2.8	54.0	361
Dutch	3.6	71.3	2.3	22.8	614
German	6.7	60.0	3.0	30.3	2,300
Italian	3.6	61.7	2.4	32.2	996
Jewish	5.3	60.8	3.3	30.6	867
Polish	7.4	56.3	4.8	31.4	726
Ukrainian	6.2	55.5	5.1	33.1	1,406
Other	5.9	55.8	3.9	34.4	3,779
Total	8.3	56.2	3.5	32.0	100
N	3,616	24,560	1,512	13,979	43,667

SOURCE: Derived from the 2% Public Census Tape obtained from the Canadian Association on Gerontology/Association Canadienne de Gerontologie.

to them for social support, confirming the data in the Canadian census (Statistics Canada 1984). The natives also see more relatives and friends every week.

Young (1984) argues this reflects a perference among native people to live in extended family settings. She cautions that this does not mean they prefer to live in the substandard housing that has been reported high among this group (Kelly 1983; Bienvenue and Havens 1986). The strains associated with increased interaction were not studied. Nevertheless, aboriginals had larger networks and interacted with them more frequently, indicating there was more potential informal support. In a similar vein, Vanderburgh (1982) argues that among reserve Indians in Canada, one or more grandparents traditionally live in the household and provide much of the socialization for the grandchildren. The elderly perform important functions for the extended family.

Chappell and Penning (1984) analyzed Winnipeg data for five ethnic groups: the British, French, German, Ukrainian and Russian, and Jews. Nonfamilial as well as familial support and relations with peers (including spouse, siblings, friends, neighbours, and confidants) and parent-child rela-

TABLE 4.1b

LIVING ARRANGEMENT BY ETHNICITY,
AGED 65 AND OVER, CANADA, 1981

(B) Living Arrangements				
Ethnic Group	Live Alone	Live with Family*	Live with Other†	N
British	29.2%	59.2%	11.6%	21,387
French	23.0	61.2	15.9	9,578
British & French	31.1	52.3	16.6	367
British & Other	32.6	56.0	11.4	525
French & Other	30.0	48.8	21.3	80
Chinese	14.5	43.9	41.6	351
Dutch	18.6	73.6	7.7	607
German	26.2	62.1	11.6	2,268
Italian	12.3	63.9	23.8	989
Jewish	27.8	62.2	10.0	863
Polish	27.0	59.7	13.2	718
Ukrainian	27.9	60.1	12.0	1,392
Other	24.3	58.2	17.5	3,727
Total	26.5	59.9	13.6	100
N	11,371	25,657	5,824	42,852

* Refers to Census family — i.e., those who live in same dwelling and have a husband/wife or parent/never-married child relationship.

† Refers to non-Census family — can include relatives and non-relatives.

SOURCE: Derived from the 2% Public Census Tape obtained from the Canadian Association on Gerontology/Association Canadienne de Gerontologie.

tionships were examined. Among the French, there seemed to be a greater access to relatives, together with fewer friends and people seen for specific purposes (instrumental relations). Even though this group reported a larger number of relatives (siblings, children, and grandchildren in particular), they also reported less frequent interaction with the large kin network. Ukrainians were the least likely to report co-residence with children, but were more likely to have sons living close by, especially in farm areas. They reported more frequent interaction with sons than with daughters. All the other ethnic groups reported more frequent interaction with daughters than with sons. Such findings suggest ethnic differences, but no clear pattern of differentiation except for the French.

Their analyses also examined individuals with Canadian ethnic identification and those who claim no ethnic identification. Neither group has received much attention in the literature. Most studies assume that lack of ethnic identification increases with the generations (an assimilationist view we do not accept). Preliminary analyses of the Winnipeg data show that the elderly who identify themselves as Canadian are no more or less likely to differ from those who claim British, French, German, Ukrainian, or Jewish identity on most of the social network variables measured. However, there are non-identifier, Canadian, Ukrainian, and Jewish differences. Non-identifiers are more likely to have larger networks available to them. They see more of their relatives who live outside of the household, but have less frequent contact with the totality of persons outside the household. They also tend to be more satisfied with their friendships, and they talk less to their neighbours. However, this group is not significantly different from British, French, or German elders with respect to the social network variables studied.

The 1981 Census provides additional information. Unfortunately, native peoples are not reported as a separate group. Information is available on ancestry for some other groups, however. As shown in Table 4.1a (p. 70) the Chinese elderly are distinctive with respect to marital status. Fewer Chinese elderly than members of the other ethnic groups are single, married, divorced, or separated. They are more likely to be widowed (54 percent). In contrast, the Dutch are least likely to be widowed (22.8 percent) and most likely to be married (71.3 percent). The British and French (whether mixed ancestry or not) are the most likely to have never married.

Elderly Chinese Canadians are also the most likely to live with someone other than a parent or unmarried child (often with other Chinese males) and least likely to live either alone or with their own family. Dutch elderly are the most likely to live with their family (expected given the percentage who are still married), the least likely to live with others, and one of the least likely to live alone. Those of British, French, or mixed British or mixed French ethnicity are the most likely to live alone (see Table 4.1b, p. 71). Number of people in the household is not shown here, but the figures reveal similar findings. The Chinese are the least likely to live with no one else in the household and the most likely (66.1 percent) to live with two or more other persons. The Dutch tend to live with only one other person (their spouse). Italian Canadians, like the Chinese, are also the least likely to live alone (12.3 percent).

Looking at number of children ever born (Table 4.2), very few elderly Italians and Chinese were childless, and they were most likely (along with the Dutch and French Canadians) to have had three or more children. Chinese elderly males in Canada were usually married, but their families were left in China.

That is, elderly Chinese emerge as somewhat distinctive. They are more likely to live as singles in Canada (married "bachelors"), living with people other than their spouse or children because their families were left in China. Elderly Dutch Canadians are more likely still to be married and living only with their spouse. Elderly British and French Canadians are more likely never to have married, to have no children, and to live alone, while elderly

TABLE 4.2

NUMBER OF CHILDREN EVER BORN BY ETHNICITY, AGED 65 AND OVER, CANADA, 1981

| Ethnic Group | Number of Children | | | | |
	0	1	2	3+	N
British	17.0%	17.0%	23.4%	42.6%	11,320
French	16.0	9.4	11.7	62.9	4,925
British & French	18.7	15.2	17.2	49.0	198
British & Other	17.8	14.4	21.6	46.2	292
French & Other	16.7	14.6	12.5	56.3	48
Chinese	5.2	11.7	22.1	61.0	213
Dutch	9.4	8.7	16.0	65.9	287
German	12.0	12.9	20.2	54.9	1,173
Italian	3.9	10.8	21.7	63.6	492
Jewish	14.8	20.1	33.3	31.9	433
Polish	12.2	17.7	22.6	47.5	345
Ukrainian	10.8	13.9	22.8	52.4	710
Other	13.8	14.5	20.3	51.4	1,950
Total	15.5	14.5	20.3	49.7	100
N	3,460	3,252	4,545	11,129	22,386

SOURCE: Derived from the 2% Public Census Tape obtained from the Canadian Association on Gerontology/Association Canadienne de Gerontologie.

Italians are more likely to live with others. Much more research is needed, especially in terms of whether or not the availability of network members translates into support. If that is the case, what types of supports do they have, and what are the accompanying strains?

Supportiveness of Ethnic Group Membership

What can be said about support networks and ethnicity, even though research is limited? Research does suggest that membership in an ethnic group can offer an important form of informal support. In addition, we know that the argument concerning the lack of an extended network among so-called whites of the general population is untrue. Similarly, the nostalgic belief in the extended family network in times past is now documented as false. Support by the extended family of preindustrial Europe and North America, in contrast to today's modified extended family, has been exposed as myth (Laslett 1976; Fischer 1978). Most research suggests that family relations have traditionally and still do provide a major source of interpersonal support and warmth for persons of all ages, including the elderly (Abu-Laban 1980). As Brody (1981) notes, research during the past several decades has systematically disproved the notion that contemporary families are alienated from the aged and do not care for them as they once did. The concept of the isolated nuclear family has been replaced by that of the modified extended family.

Most elderly have fairly extensive contact with their children (Shanas 1979). The maintenance of close family ties while living separately geographically is well described by the phrase *intimacy-at-a-distance* (Rosenmayr and Kockeis 1963). Most elderly persons with children live close to at least one child and often see at least one on a regular basis. Canadian data from the Hamilton area in Ontario (Rosenthal 1986) show that only 11 percent of older people (age 70 and over) who have children live more than one and a half hours away from the nearest child. Interaction with children is, however, mediated through proximity (Heltsley and Powers 1975).

Informal networks include friends, neighbours, and other non-family members, as well as family. Hochschild (1973) reports evidence of a "sibling bond" among elderly residents of a subsidized apartment building. She also reports that those who interact most actively with children are also most actively involved with non-kin. Canadian data from Winnipeg (Chappell 1983) reveal that contact with individuals outside the household is more frequent with friends (who are primarily age peers) than with relatives or neighbours. Further, more satisfaction is expressed with relating to friends than with any others outside the household. More research is required on kin and non-kin interactions.

That is, generally speaking, we know that the modified extended family exists today and that most elderly people are not isolated and alienated from their family and friends. The variability in informal support that exists by ethnicity is, however, largely unknown. Which ethnic groups have more or less extensive ties and the circumstances that lead to these conditions is not known. Similarly, it is not known which ethnic groups offer the elderly what types of support and under what circumstances. We expect elderly Indian, Chinese, Dutch, British, and French Canadians to show variations in terms of informal networks in future research. In terms of modernization and pluralism, discussed earlier, it is not clear that either modernization or assimilation leads to decreases in the amounts or types of familial or non-familial support. It is highly likely that the types of support change over time and are affected by the composition of the group, immigration history, economic resources, and so forth.

In terms of the types of ethnic elders proposed in Chapter 3, it will be recalled that supportiveness of family and groups ties was expected for most groups, including the native Indians, European prairie farmers, the French charter minority, the various British types, and the Jewish moderns. The question therefore becomes, do the types of support vary by ethnic group and in which ways? To some extent, available evidence supports the notion of the aboriginal pre-modern type, demonstrating a tendency for extended family settings, larger networks outside as well as inside the household, and more interaction with members of their networks. However, we do not know the extent to which natives prefer these situations or whether they primarily reflect economic necessity and a lack of available alternatives. Strains and stresses associated with such situations are largely unresearched.

It was expected that European prairie farm elders within a multicultural setting would also have solid family and group support. Empirical verification is by and large lacking. The Chinese elderly seem to have people available to assist them, they tend to live in large households, and to live with people other than spouses or children. What type of support is linked to strong ethnic ties? Do the Jewish elderly tend to live in more expensive institutions among their ethnic peers but have fewer options to remain in the community by themselves living close to their families or friends?

Despite the lack of information on ethnic variation in informal support, existing data suggest that ethnicity is an important factor to consider. The native, Chinese, British, and French elderly all show important differences in their informal support. That is, ethnic culture can be important to consider when social policy is a concern. Contrary to modernization and assimilation theories, ethnicity can have significant implications for care and supportiveness in old age, implications to be taken into account in addition to socioeconomic status and mobility.

It should be noted that cultural variations in the meaning of words pose special problems in this area. For example, Strain and Chappell (1984) caution that the large number of friends reported by native elderly may reflect their tendency to call acquaintances friends. This is the same problem Sterne et al. (1974, as reported in Creecy and Wright 1979) report in their study of the friendships of the black elderly. They indicate that the black elderly embrace a loose conception of friendship and in many instances consider casual acquaintances friends. The white elderly, in contrast, delineate their interpersonal world more precisely and confine their friendships to intimate relationships. That is, the definition and meaning of *friend* and *friendship*, like so many words, is culture bound (Cohen and Rajkowski 1982). Such cultural differences must be taken into account when studying ethnic variations.

FORMAL SERVICES: AN ETHNIC DISADVANTAGE?

If the literature suggests advantages for the minority and ethnic elderly in terms of informal support, it also suggests a lack of utilization of formal services. The *Canadian Government Report on Aging* (Begin 1982) believes a person's cultural background can impede the receipt of needed services. Morrison (1983) argues the utilization of long-term care facilities by the minority aged has never been great. Greene and Monahan (1984) find the

Hispanic utilize disproportionately small amounts of formal long-term care services compared with the Anglo elderly. The reason offered is twofold: the higher rates of informal support and exclusion from mainstream services.

Once again, much of the research is American. Guttman (1979) studied the white ethnic aged, including Estonians, Greeks, Hungarians, Italians, Jews, Latvians, Lithuanians, and two groups of Poles. Ethnic friends, and to a large degree ethnic organizations, are preferred to any other support system. Cuellar (1981) studied Mexican Americans (chicanos) and Anglos and reported that chicanos use alternate sources of support, such as family networks, folk healers, priests, ministers, and general practitioners rather than professional mental health services.

Kim (1983) writes that many Chinese and Korean American elderly feel comfortable with and use organic folk medicines. They are distrustful of chemical-synthetic medicines. The fact that such community resources are available may lead to the underuse of traditional mental health services by these individuals. That is, the underutilization of such services may be directly related to such culturally relevant alternative kinds of mental health care within the community. In addition, Wu (1975) argues that language barriers and culture shock have separated the Chinese elderly from mainstream society and excluded them from receiving needed services, more than is true of the elderly in general.

Others have questioned this view, arguing that virtually all elderly lack adequate services, not simply the ethnic elderly (Kalish and Yuen 1971). Studying a community that was heavily Catholic, Polish, and working class, Biegel and Sherman (1979) report that neither age nor ethnicity mattered much in terms of whether or not an individual sought help for a problem. Source of referral, cost of the service, and location of the service in the neighbourhood were the most significant factors related to seeking help. Further, most elderly meet their social and daily needs within a six-block radius of their home. Present helping networks, communities and professions, are internally fragmented, they frequently operate separately rather than in a comprehensive, co-ordinated effort. For example, more often than not, social services and health services are delivered through different branches of government with different funding and reporting lines.

Still other studies suggest the negative relationship posed between informal and formal care is not warranted. Starrett and associates (1983) studied the Hispanic elderly and found that those interacting more with kin, friends, and neighbours were more likely to be aware of social services designed to meet their needs and to consume more services. These data suggest that those more actively involved in informal networks are more likely to use formal services as well. This is consistent with literature on the broker role (Lin 1982), arguing that one of the advantages of weak ties as opposed to strong ties is their linkage to dissimilar individuals and therefore access to information or influence not otherwise available (McKinlay 1973).

Similarly, Mindel and Wright (1982) report that informal assistance to the elderly is not an alternative to aid from institutional sources, but is a supplement to seeking help from outside sources. Canadian data from Winnipeg suggest that for the elderly in general, the use of home care services is a complement to informal assistance and that the two are not mutually exclusive (Chappell 1985). Among the elderly in Winnipeg, about 15 percent living in the community are also receiving some type of formal care. Eighty percent who receive formal care also receive informal assistance at the same time (Chappell and Havens 1985).

In addition, recent studies from the United States suggest that members of ethnic groups are not opposed to formal care as is sometimes assumed. Gelfand and Fandetti (1980) studied middle-aged, Italian American males in a suburban area and compared them with working class, inner-city Italians and Poles. They report that persons in the suburbs are more likely to accept nursing home care for bedridden relatives and are less concerned about the ethnicity of the care provider. They argue that the acceptance of institutional services by the high income, college-educated suburban sample reflected their ability to pay for alternative forms of care. They also note it may indicate a belief that there is more assurance of obtaining high quality services from the private sector. They argue that this choice will be most evident among the more well-to-do white ethnics and those not raised in a minority neighbourhood. Whether this is due to greater access to finances or a greater geographic and psychological distance associated with a different lifestyle is not known (Cantor 1979; Gelfand 1982, 97).

Among inner-city Italians and Poles, Fandetti and Gelfand (1976) report that intergenerational households are favoured for the ambulatory and bedridden aged relatives. However, this preference is weaker among second- and third-generation respondents than for first-generation peers, presumably because for some, ethnic ties have weakened. It was also weaker among those with higher educational and income levels. Gelfand (1982, 61) argues that high educational levels account for more varied interethnic experiences. Where elderly relatives require intensive medical care, many are willing to utilize long-term care facilities. The respondents, also, did not display attitudes of suspicion toward outgroup caretakers from the larger society. For most, competency and professionalism appeared to be the major determinants of attitudes toward caretakers working with the elderly in the community. The Poles, however, were more likely to provide a postitive evaluation of nurses who were not indigenous to the local community, suggesting some ethnic variation.

There is, at the same time, evidence of ethnic variations in the utilization of specific services. Berk and Bernstein (1982) note variations by the service considered. They report that non-white elderly are more likely than the white elderly to receive care in institutional settings rather than in physicians' offices. The white elderly are more likely to have a regular source of care that provides housecalls and emergency services. Lower life expectancies of minority aged, and of minority aged males in particular, can result in a decrease in the risk of institutionalization. Canadian aboriginal life expectancies are approximately 20 years lower than other Canadians. Morrison (1983) argues that the minority aged who are not in immediate family situations are more prone to institutionalization.

Although utilization of formal services by the ethnic elderly is receiving increased attention in the United States, it is still a relatively new area. Lack of resolution of problems reflects the state of this research. Some support exists for the position that ethnic groups are less likely to use the formal system, for both push and pull reasons, exclusionary factors within the system and available informal support. Sufficient evidence does exist for us to know that the relationship with ethnicity is diverse and complex. In some instances, extended informal networks can increase utilization of certain aspects of the formal system. We turn now to the Canadian experience.

Some Canadian Evidence

In Canada, the provision of health care is a provincial responsibility, although national insurance coverage is in place for physician's services and hospital utilization. That is, the emphasis in the health care system is distinctly medical and institutional. Services for chronic care in the community are not nearly as well developed. Of relevance here is the fact that most elderly suffer from chronic conditions, not acute episodes, and prefer to remain in familiar surroundings in the community, not in long-term institutional care. This section on utilization therefore must be understood in the context of a health care system that may not be the most appropriate to meet the needs of the elderly. (See Chappell et al. 1986, for a detailed discussion of the Canadian system and its appropriateness for an aging population.)

The problem is confounded by the dearth of data on utilization of services by ethnicity. There is less research on the use of formal services than on informal supports. Apparently one of the reasons for the lack of such data by ethnicity is the sensitivity of the topic and potential for misinterpretation. Nevertheless, some information is available. We report here on most types of income and health care services: government income transfer programs, such as the old age security payment and the guaranteed income supplement; collective households that include but are not restricted to long-term care institutions; and local data on home care utilization, physician's visits, hospital stays, and institutional care.

Two Canadian studies examine ethnic variation by participation in government programs. Wanner and McDonald (1984) studied men and women aged 55 to 65 and found that Asians, Africans, and Latin Americans of both genders are less likely to be out of the labour force collecting old age security payments, Canada Pension, or Quebec Pension. Women are more likely to remain in the labour force than men. For both genders, there is a distinct dichotomy between the Canadian and European born, and those born in Third World regions, with the latter less likely to receive social insurance benefits. Only one-half to one-third as many Third World women receive old age security payments, Canada Pension, or Quebec Pension as Canadian or European-born women 65 and over. They find, however, that the effects of ethnicity on income are minor at best. Hum and Chan (1980) report that the take-up rate for old age security-guaranteed income supplement among the Chinese in Winnipeg is low, due they argue, to their low cultural and structural assimilation into Canadian society.

Other data indicate ethnic variations in the use of health services. Winnipeg native Indians aged 50 and over use home care services to a lesser extent than others (Young 1984). Only .5 percent report ever having received home care services such as homemaker services and only 6 percent having had nursing services at home. However, 15 percent of all the elderly receive such services in Winnipeg. Just as many native Indians use physician's services (80 percent) as other elderly 65 and over (85 percent).

Census data (Statistics Canada 1981) show variations in type of residence by mother tongue. Unfortunately, long-term care institutions are not categorized separately. When collective households are defined to include hotels, motels, rooming houses, hospitals and correctional institutions, as well as special care homes and nursing homes for the elderly and chronically ill, French-speaking elderly are the most likely (12.1 percent) to live in such households; English- Greek- and Chinese-speaking elderly rank next (8.5 percent, 8.7 percent and 8.4 percent, respectively). The Portuguese-speaking elderly are the least likely (2.5 percent) to reside in collective dwellings, followed by the Dutch (3.4 percent) and Italians (3.6 percent). Looking at inmates of institutions (consisting primarily but not entirely of nursing homes), Stone and Fletcher (1985) report that among those age 60 and over, those belonging to a third language group (i.e., not English or French mother tongue) are least likely to reside in institutions. Although there tend to be one or at most two studies in each area, the reality of under-utilization by specific groups is clear.

Further, a Manitoba study (Shapiro and Roos 1981; Mossey et al. 1981) does provide provincial data for 1977 on type of residence, used here to examine long-term institutional care. It is clear from Table 4.3 that there is some variation by ethnicity. Canadian identifiers tend to be in mental and extended care hospitals, while the British tend not to be in such institutions. The British, however, are likely to reside in hostels. Russians and Ukrainians tend to reside in the community, in personal care homes, or mental, extended care hospitals but not in housing units or hostels.

Data reviewed here do not address the question whether services are ade-

TABLE 4.3

ETHNICITY BY TYPE OF RESIDENCE, MANITOBA, 1977

	Type of Residence				
Ethnicity	Community	Housing Unit	Hostel	P.C.H.	Mental/ Extended Hospital
Canadian	9%	9%	8%	8%	21%
American (USA)	1	1	1	1	1
British	42	47	56	46	35
French	5	10	6	7	4
German	8	11	10	6	9
Norwegian/Danish/ Swedish/Icelandic	5	7	9	6	3
Dutch/Belgian	3	7	2	4	1
Polish	5	2	—	3	6
Russian/Ukrainian	15	5	7	16	15
Other European	3	1	0	3	6
Asia Oceanic	0	—	0	0	—
Native	3	—	—	0	—
Total Percent	99	100	99	100	101
Total N	3,532	372	213	418	164

SOURCE: Computed from the Aging in Manitoba data set; for details concerning this study see J. M. Mossey, B. Havens, N. P. Roos, and E. Shapiro, "The Manitoba Longitudinal Study on Aging: Description and Methods," The Gerontologist, 1981, 21:551–58.

quate to meet needs, but only whether there is variation in utilization of those services that exist. It would appear that service utilization does vary by ethnicity, but many more studies with sensitive measuring instruments are needed. Those from Third World countries underutilize income security programs. Native Indians underutilize home care services. It will be important in future research to examine informal supports that complement or substitute for formal services within ethnic groups. Information on needs is also critical in order to assess the implications of differences found between groups. The question of need is addressed next.

Cumulative Disadvantages

Besides culture, there is an additional argument for why ethnicity is important in the delivery of services. Disadvantage among specific ethnic groups suggests they may be more in need of specific services than are other groups. The extent to which racial, ethnic, or cultural factors influence patterns of health, longevity, and poverty relates to whether racial or ethnic minority aged will be more at risk and more in need of certain types of care than other aged. Many authors argue that discrimination and poverty experienced when young results in additional disadvantage when reaching old age (Kim 1983; Morrison 1983). The double or triple jeopardy hypothesis (Chappell and Havens 1980) is relevant here.

The importance of health as people age cannot be disputed. It is to a large extent deteriorating health in old age that is the reason for concern related to increases in dependency or lack of self-sufficiency. The rising proportions of elderly individuals and the expected demand on the health care system as a result of their deteriorating health has engendered concern among policy makers, politicians, and others.

According to the Canada Health Survey of 1978/79 (Health and Welfare Canada 1981), only 14.4 percent of those aged 65 and over living in the community report no health problems (including both acute and chronic conditions). Fully 85.6 percent had at least one health problem. The elderly also report more health problems than younger adults. Nearly one-half (48.7 percent) of the adults less than 65 years of age, as reported in the Canada Health Survey, have no chronic conditions, while 51.3 percent report one or more. However, 85 percent of elderly individuals (65 plus) in Canada report some chronic conditions. This need not mean that there are limitations on activity or that there is functional disability. Among those age 65 and over, 61.8 percent report no limitations on their activity (Chappell et al. 1986). The figure is even higher if only those limitations that are severe or affect major activities are included; the figure cited is usually over 80 percent (Branch and Jette 1981). On the other hand, the Canada Health Survey reveals that fully 91 percent of adults less than age 65 years of age are disability-free.

Furthermore, concern surrounding loss of intellectual capacity as age increases is longstanding. This is commonly referred to as dementia. Alzheimer's disease accounts for approximately half of all people with dementia, and it is more common among elderly individuals than younger adults (Eisdorfer and Cohen 1982). The likelihood of dementia increases with age (Pitt 1982), although it is difficult to know the exact figures because of problems with diagnoses (best estimates suggest 5 to 6 percent of those aged 65 and over suffer from dementia). Other areas of mental or psychological health, however, are not likely to worsen as age increases. For example, depression, while a problem among a significant minority of elderly persons, is most prevalent in younger adults (Hirshfeld and Cross 1982; Amenson and Lewinshon 1981). This is confirmed in a recent Canadian study (Barnes and Chappell 1982) that shows a negative correlation between age and depression.

Subjective perceptions of health are usually better than actual measures of disease and disability. Wolinsky (1983) reports that less than one-third (30.2 percent) of the elderly 85 and over report poor or fair health in the United States. Most elderly persons report good or excellent health. Comparable national data are not available in Canada, but Manitoba data suggest similar trends. Less than one-third (29.4 percent) of the elderly in Winnipeg (Chappell 1983) say their health is fair or poor. More information is available on global indicators of happiness than perceived health, per se. The Canada Health Survey does reveal that few elderly persons score negatively on Bradburns's Affect Balance Scale (7.1 percent), with many more in the positive category (53.3 percent).

The effects of deteriorating health, often leading to death, are profound. Linn and associates (1979) report that degree of physical disability is most associated with adjustment, more so than social class or ethnicity. Nevertheless, ethnic differences in degree of health are evident. Satariano and associates (1982) studied cancer incidence rates among black and white Americans. They report that black women are particularly at risk of cervical cancer, and middle-aged black men of multiphasic cancer. In Canada, Hassan et al. (1978) report a higher risk of mortality from ischemic heart disease than expected among the Jews, English, and Scottish in Manitoba. There was a lower risk among the native Indians, Austrians, Germans, and Ukrainians.

Kalish and Yuen (1971) report that Japanese Americans are exceptionally healthy and their longevity is high. Linn et al. (1979) report that blacks are significantly less depressed and have better self-concepts than either elderly whites or Cubans, and that elderly whites have less self-esteem. However, they also report the variable most associated with adjustment is degree of physical disability. Markides et al. (1981) report that health has a strong independent effect on life satisfaction among Mexican Americans. Morrison (1983) notes that non-whites compared to whites have poorer self-reported health status and noticeably more chronic conditions and disabilities.

There is also evidence that poverty is related to ill health. Generally, the lower the socioeconomic status, the higher the prevalence of disease, the higher the functional disability, and the higher the age-specific death rate (Shanas and Maddox 1976; Evans 1984). Further, for many of the conditions experienced by the disadvantaged, health education and preventive measures would do much to reduce illness and death caused by them, since many are related to poor personal health care, inadequate diet, and smoking and alcohol consumption.

Health indicators by ethnicity are difficult to find in Canada. There is no periodic national health survey in this country as there is in the United States. The Canada Health Survey, conducted in 1978/79, provides data on the number of chronic conditions, activity limitation, and the number of visits to a physician by mother tongue. However, this survey groups the information broadly as English, French, and other, without further distinctions. No significant differences emerge using such general demarcations.

Some information on native Canadians is available. The Winnipeg study of long-time native residents aged 50 and over (Young 1984; Strain and

Chappell 1984), referred to earlier, provides comparative data for those aged 65 and over living in Winnipeg. These Winnipeg data suggest the health of Indians deteriorates earlier than non-natives, probably due to life-long poverty and disadvantage. Native Canadians at birth have a life expectancy approximately 20 years lower than non-natives. Those who live to be 50 still have a lower life expectancy. They have a higher prevalence of diseases, notably tuberculosis and diabetes (Health and Welfare Canada 1984). Indians living in Winnipeg aged 50 and over show health levels similar to non-natives aged 65 and over when assessed in terms of chronic conditions, functional disability, and days stayed in hospitals. Realistically, they are also more likely to consider their health poor or bad when compared with others (19 percent versus 7.8 percent).

There is, in other words, sufficient information to suggest that differences in health by ethnicity are real. However, except for native Indians, insufficient data exist to compare specific needs and services that may result from health differences. One major obstacle in this area is the lack of periodic national surveys. Another is the lack of data for specific ethnic groups.

SUMMARY

We have noted at the outset of this chapter that high socioeconomic status and other indicators of mobility are not necessarily correlated with assimilation. Increasingly, scholars (Darroch 1979; Tepperman 1975; Isajiw and Driedger 1986) find that the relationship between ethnic identity and social mobility is not as simplistic and unilinear as assimilationists have suggested. Evidence reviewed earlier in the book confirmed this position. It was further suggested that not all elderly necessarily lose status once they enter old age, although clearly more research is required in this area. More important for this discussion, we argued that the reason for high status, but simultaneously maintaining ethnic identity, is to be found within small group relations and ethnic culture. It is within ethnic culture that individuals learn their norms of behaviour and their interpretations of the world in which they live. While a distinct lack of data on maintaining ethnic identity among Canada's elderly was noted, nevertheless much of the gerontological literature in this area does deal with supportive relations among ethnic groups for their elderly members. This literature is relevant to the discussion of ethnic culture and is also pragmatically concerned with assistance during old age when health deteriorates. That is, it has direct policy and practitioner relevance.

Next we proceeded to review the information available on supportive primary-group relations for elderly individuals who belong to ethnic groups and concomitantly on their utilization of the formal care system. While more research is needed, it is clear that ethnicity can be important for the provision of informal support. This appears evident despite the ongoing debate in the literature about whether the relationships with ethnicity might be explained by socioeconomic status. The lack of information is especially evident in terms of the utilization of the formal care system, but the evidence available again suggests ethnic variation. A major question here is whether or not the current health care system is designed to meet adequately the needs of the elderly. If it is not, the usefulness of looking at utilization rates without also examining needs can be questioned. By reviewing informal and formal support, this chapter has examined care for etn-elders at both a small-group and macro (institutional) level.

Particularly lacking, as is evident throughout all of the chapters in this book, are studies of the social-psychological level, examining the process of interpretation at the individual level. Without denying the influences of modernization or its impact on the elderly, there is good reason to believe that these processes do not have the impact implied in the modernization and assimilation theories. We suggest that while larger societal forces, such as exclusion from paid labour, have profound influences on the elderly, by and large they act as a context for individual adjustment in later life. Primary-group relations and other day-to-day features are used to interpret the meaning and relevance of the larger forces for the individual. Life for the most part goes on and salient features emerge that are different when one is retired than they are when one is engaged in full-time labour. In other words, the worlds of the retired and the nonretired can differ substantially, and additional studies are required to understand the world of the retired from their own point of view.

Evidence in support of this view is found in Roadburg's (1985) study of leisure among a group of elderly persons in Nova Scotia. Roadburg notes that retirement is usually equated with leisure because leisure is tied to the meaning of work. He suggests that such a definition is inappropriate for the study of leisure among the elderly. For the elderly, leisure must be disassociated from the concept of paid labour because most elderly are not in paid labour. In contrast to most studies of working people, where freedom is considered a major component of leisure, the retirees studied by Roadburg tended to define leisure in terms of enjoyment and relaxation. Over 80 percent of them said that all day was free time, so it is not surprising that freedom was no longer a distinguishing feature of their leisure.

An anthropoligical study by Keith (1980) also supports this view. As Fry (1980, 171) has noted, Keith demonstrates how old people can and do create their own communities. These communities, frequently branded "old folks homes" or "geriatric ghettos" by outsiders (usually younger), are filled with the people, events, and emotions of their residents' lives. Outsiders frequently do not see the world within, factors important to these people, or the forces impinging on them. Keith reports that in one residence she studied, external sources of status (prestige) were quite simply irrelevant. Instead, it was those participating most in resident affairs, either formal or informal, who were accorded highest status. Within their world, sharing (relationships that involve interdependence) resolves around three types of activities: assistance when ill or disabled, reciprocity of goods, and socio-emotional friendship ties.

We suggest, therefore, that economic status and the older person's relationship to the means of production is probably not of paramount importance in his or her day-to-day life. Available Canadian data suggest the factors identified here often vary in important ways by ethnicity. Native Indians emerge as a distinctive group, irrespective of dimensions examined, although more information is needed to show in what ways the social network is supportive and in what ways Indian culture is changing. Information on European prairie farm elders, on their adjustment to old age, and on the extent to which their ethnic culture is relevant is also required. While we hear much about Jewish homes for the aged, notably Baycrest Centre in Toronto, we do not know the proportion of Jewish elderly in such homes, the living arrangements of Jewish elders not in such homes, and the stresses associated with different types of accommodation.

Having reviewed existing knowledge of informal and formal support, in the next, concluding chapter we will continue the discussion of social policy concerns; an explicit review of social policy for eth-elders is presented.

CHAPTER 5

POLICY CONSIDERATIONS

Throughout the discussion of aging and ethnicity, we have argued for the relevance of ethnicity for eth-elder social policy. In this chapter, social policy is the focus. First, the issue of need versus age is raised, followed by a discussion of various components that satisfy needs. Eth-elder types are than specifically discussed.

ETH-ELDER NEEDS AND SOCIAL POLICY

Age Versus Need

Current social policies sometimes designate age as the eligibility criterion. The old age security payment, for example, is given to everyone age 65 and over. Other programs are based on economic need. The guaranteed income supplement is provided to those individuals age 65 and over whose total income falls below a specified amount. Still other benefits are based on other kinds of needs. The services of medical specialists, various medical laboratory tests, and prescription drugs are provided only when assessed as required by physicians.

When services for the elderly are to be provided, a basic decision must be made concerning eligibility. Will anyone of a given age receive aid or will an assessment of need be made? Social policies based on age have many proponents who argue that the disproportionate number of old persons living in poverty, having poor health, and receiving inadequate medical and health care means old people as a group should be targeted for programming. Proponents argue that such policies will ensure a redistribution of social resources. Without such policies, structural inequalities and ageist attitudes will force a continuation of these inequities (Neugarten 1982a; 1982b). Such policies have the added advantage of being administratively efficient and relatively unobtrusive. Further, it has been shown that the public is in favour of provision of life-supporting services to the elderly in areas such as income and nutrition (Kutza and Zweibel 1982). Finally, proponents argue that universal policies prevent the stigma associated with means-tested services.

Opponents to age-based programming point out that the circumstances and status of the elderly have improved sufficiently that age-based policies now provide services to those who do not need them. As a consequence, they argue, the elderly poor and frail have their needs only partially rather than adequately met. Branch (1980) argues that between 15 to 20 percent of the elderly require special services, and their needs become masked by the 80 to 85 percent who do not require such services. In other words, age is not (or is no longer) a valid predictor of need. Furthermore, many argue that assessment for services due to declining health does not hold the same stigma as economic means tests, which are frequently associated with being unworthy and morally inferior. There is a tendency to view sickness as something that happens without personal responsibility, so that an individual in need of health services will not be stigmatized.

Our discussion of aging and ethnicity suggests that it is more appropriate to provide according to need than according to age alone. Needs will vary depending on such factors as the extent of the person's ethnic identification, the prevalence of services that are ethnically congruent, the health of the individual, the social support available to the person, and the individual's ability and style of coping. This is in no way an argument against universality or accessibility of services. Services should be available for all of those in need. There is no doubt, however, that provision of services on the basis of need is much more problematic, because the definition and measurement of *need* is multifaceted. Needs can refer to traditional health and medical needs, as well as housing, transportation, nutrition, and socio-emotional needs, to name a few. After needs are specified and defined, one has to decide how they are to be measured. Then they have to be translated into a care plan or package of services (Austin and Loeb 1982). Need-based policies, further, require skilled personnel for proper implementation, accomplished through "target efficient" programs, unlike services provided to everyone on the basis of age alone.

Meeting the Needs of Eth-elders

There is much literature that recognizes the special needs of different ethnic groups stemming from their unique ethno-history, language, and culture, and the importance of incorporating these elements into service delivery systems (Cueller 1981). Even reports of the Canadian government (Begin 1982) recognize that "familiar cultural surroundings" may be important in the provision of services.

The paramount importance of language is unmistakable in MacLean and Bonar's (1983) descriptions of elderly residents of a long-term care institution in Montreal. The residents described could not speak English or French; no one else could speak their language; and mental and physical devastation was the result. The role of culture is evident in Ujimoto's (1986) work on Japanese elders. He tells how they tend not to express pain and suffering because it is a sign of weakness; elderly Asians regard doctors as authority figures, and consequently, they seldom question doctors directly. Another example comes from Strong's (1984) study comparing Indian and white caregivers of elderly relatives. The Indians' greater belief in "passive forbearance," together with a cultural dictum forbidding interference, differed dramatically from the white group.

Many advocate that services be delivered by members of the ethnic group (Krickus 1980). If this is not possible, agency personnel can work with members of that community. Grassroots social service programs designed, based, and implemented in and by the community are often mentioned. Informing ethnic individuals about the services is insufficient. Providing services withing their cultural context is of major importance. This argument also applies to long-term care. Morrison (1983), for example, notes that the utilization of nursing homes by minority aged is higher if facilities are located inside ethnic neighbourhoods. Not only must neighbourhood location be considered in long-term care, but culturally accustomed patterns of eating, socializing, and living in general must also be taken into consideration. That is, cultural congruence is important where ethnic culture is sufficiently distinct to warrant attention.

The native elderly in Winnipeg are seeking such services (Chappell and Strain 1984). They have a overwhelming preference for services that are designed, co-ordinated, and facilitated by Indians. They want consideration given to cultural preferences, and they want to be able to communicate in their own language. Table 5.1 shows that 58 percent say there is considerable or extreme need for public social services to be provided in their own language and by native people. Fully 85 percent say there is at least some need. Over three-quarters (78 percent) report the importance of living among people of their own cultural background, and over half (60 percent) would like more opportunity to use their own language.

Chan's (1983) study of elderly Chinese women in Montreal demonstrates the importance of the community and the culture in service delivery. The women in her study knew and used services located in Chinatown. They even used these agencies for assistance in filling out government forms for subsidies. There was, however, no indication they used or even knew about services outside the Chinese community. Wolf and associates (1983) note that working class elders, irrespective of ethnicity, meet most of their social and daily needs within the neighbourhood. That is, most of us, whether members of an ethnic group or not, prefer familiar surroundings, customary food, and individualized service. Why should eth-elders who have distinctive cultural values be any different?

Many charge that the insensitivity of agency personnel to cultural nuances is one of the reasons members of ethnic groups underutilize agency services (Kim 1983; Lum 1983; Wesley-King 1983). Whether this insensitivity stems from the belief on the part of agency personnel that members of ethnic groups are well cared for by their families, from ignorance, from

TABLE 5.1

PREFERENCE FOR CULTURALLY RELEVANT SERVICES, INDIANS AGED 50 AND OVER, WINNIPEG, 1984

	N	%
Public social services should be provided in own language and by native persons.		
No, little need	27	15
Some	49	27
Considerable/extreme need	103	58
	179	100
Importance of living among people of own cultural background.		
Not important	40	22
Moderately important	70	38
Very important	74	40
	184	100
Would like more opportunity to use own language.		
No	31	18
Wouldn't make much difference	36	21
Yes, somewhat	41	24
Yes, very much	60	36
	168	99

SOURCE: Computed from N. L. Chappell and L. A. Strain, *Needs Assessment of Natives 50+ Living in Winnipeg* (Study conducted through the Centre on Aging, University of Manitoba, Winnipeg, 1984).

prejudice, or from ethnocentrism on the part of personnel, is not known. It need not necessarily result from prejudice and discrimination. However, lack of knowledge about a culture and/or insensitivity to cultural nuances on the part of service personnel can be as devastating in their consequences as prejudice and discrimination.

Not only is there a general call for culturally relevant services, but for increased control by members of the ethnic group as well (Bastida 1983). Watson (1983) has demonstrated that it is usually those with higher formal educational levels and social awareness who best negotiate complex organizations. Because of current cohort differences, it is frequently younger members of a group who can best manage complex organizations. The elderly working with younger members may therefore fare better than the elderly working alone. Among the elderly, we would expect the Jews would be in a better position than native Indians to influence the system, because of increased education and greater social awareness, and also because of greater economic resources.

While most writers argue for ethnically oriented services, this is by no means the only position. Indeed, Biegel and Sherman (1979) found that for a Catholic, Polish and working class community, referral by clergy, family, or a doctor was a key in the decision to seek professional assistance, irrespective of ethnicity. Who provided the service and what the ethnic background of the service provider was mattered little. More research is needed on the circumstances in which ethnicity is important and those in which it is not.

Further, many of the recommendations found in the literature on the ethnic elderly would be equally welcome among other elderly. For example, in relation to the eth-elders, Gelfand and Kutzik (1979) recommend that family therapy be a more integral part of mental health services. Particularly in the mental health area, diagnostic labels and standardized norms have been criticized as being culturally biased. In addition, Blau and associates (1979) argue for strategies to encourage the elderly to replenish and restore informal social networks of support as their social resources become depleted. The recommendation that transportation be provided not merely to visit doctors and hospitals, nutrition centres, and community centres, but also to visit friends, libraries, museums, classes, and hobby groups would be welcomed by most groups of elderly.

Indeed, the similarity of recommendations made by both ethnic scholars and gerontological scholars is striking. Kammerman (1976) reviewed services for aged individuals in eight countries (Canada, the Federal Republic of Germany, France, Israel, Poland, the United Kingdom, the United States, and Yugoslavia) and concluded that needs are fairly uniform within these countries. A common theme is that services should be designed to enable elderly persons to remain in their own homes for as long as possible. A spectrum of services required to meet the needs of the elderly and to enable them to remain in the community included: community services, multifacility or multifunction living and care complexes, congregate or sheltered housing, and long-term care facilities for the frail elderly. Coward (1979) and Beattie (1976) also argue for a similar continuum of care for elderly persons. The importance of transportation is recognized for all elderly, irrespective of ethnicity (Carp 1979; Begin 1982).

The fact that services recommended for those with high ethnic identity are similar to those needed by all elderly does not mean ethnic culture should be ignored in the provision of services. Rather, it means providing services that are familiar, within our system of beliefs, may well require attention to ethnic culture. The elderly are a heterogeneous group, and ethnicity is an important dimension to be taken into account in service delivery. Eth-elders want continuity and familiarity throughout their old age, just as do those of us for whom ethnicity is not as salient.

A question that remains unanswered is, to what extent should the form and content of services vary from one group to another? For example, when studying East European women and the family, Krickus (1980) notes that East European women generally do not confide in outsiders and are hesitant to seek outside help. They are afraid of a loss of status and self-esteem, and that others might see them as unable to cope. They exhibit a great attachment to their home, and a great resistance to succumbing to illness. Given such an attitude, homes or apartments for senior citizens could be inappropriate for these women. Programs such as visiting nurses, travelling librairies, homemaking, and meal projects might, however, be feasible.

Cuellar (1981) provides another example. This author notes an important cultural difference between Mexicans and Anglo Americans in that the Mexican culture does not separate psychological or emotional disorders from somatic diseases. In addition, it is believed that somatic diseases can have unnatural or supernatural causes. These differing views of illness can provide important clues for health professionals attempting to deliver traditional mental health services to chicanos.

How do we ensure culturally appropriate services? When the group is sufficiently distinct and identifiable and when sufficient numbers make it feasible, control by the ethnic group is an obvious strategy. This avoids the problem of educating service providers with culturally appropriate knowledge. Integrating staff, volunteers, and peer counsellors from the ethnic group can help ensure culturally relevant services. This, however, is not always possible. When it is not, and when ethnicity should be taken into account, there are several factors to be considered. They should be taken into account not only when developing general programming, but also when assessing the needs of particular individuals. All of them can be subsumed under the notion of community.

The Importance of Community

A community is a group of people interacting with one another in ways that satisfy many of their daily needs, in a system of interdependent relationships. It is a focus for group identification and frequently, but not always, forms a geographic and economic unit. However, a group of persons sharing common traditions and interests can be considered a community without sharing a common geographical area (such as a community of scholars). Members of an ethnic group can share beliefs, expectations, and behaviours even though they do not live close to one another. The concept of community, however, does imply a group identification, a feeling of shared common interests, goals, and beliefs.

The concept of community is frequently tied to ethnicity. Indeed, agency location and visibility, together with the territorial orientation of the group, have been discussed as important elements in the provision of services. Ortega and associates (1983) note that blacks' patterns of church-related affiliation are usually not taken into account in urban renewal efforts. Neighbourhood patterns of church and religious participation are then disrupted. Kahana and Felton (1977) report community of residence and living arrangements as the most important factors in a willingness to report problems. That is, the community or neighbourhood may be necessary for understanding service needs and vulnerabilities.

If the community is rural or the members of the ethnic group are dispersed, special problems are involved. Most notable is the transportation problem, which can result in reduced mobility and isolation from meaningful social contacts and relevant organizations (Gerber 1983). When studying American natives, John (1985) reported differences between natives living on reservations and those living in urban areas. The reservation native people experienced substantially more deprivation than their urban counterparts. They were poorer, supported more people on their income, had fewer social contacts, had lower life satisfaction, and were in poorer health. In particular, lack of transportation was cited as a major problem. In contrast, urban natives require services typical of an urban environment, including support and counselling. Bienvenue and Havens (1986) studied Indians living in rural Manitoba (on farms and in small towns, most of whom lived on reservations). They report that Indians have serious disadvantages in housing conditions, medical, nursing, and dental care when compared with nonnatives also living in rural areas.

If the community is multicultural, as many are on the prairies, domination of a service by any one group may be undesirable. One strategy is to build a pool of resource persons from the community who can be called upon when needed. This can work in large as well as smaller centres. For example, one of the central core area hospitals in Toronto provides a language aid system in more than 30 languages on a continuous basis. These services are available in their outpatient clinic and plans are underway to start a long-term care institution reflecting such multicultural policies. Multicultural characteristics do not, of course, prohibit specialized services for one group when their numbers warrant it. This is evident in the urban centres on the prairies. Winnipeg, for example, has Jewish personal care homes, Ukrainian personal care homes, and Mennonite facilities.

Taking community into account requires more study of the community's salient characteristics and of the indicators planners should be taking into account. It requires not only building senior's complexes close to grocery stores, doctors' offices, and the like, but also locating appropriate accommodation within the community, so that elders who wish to do so can remain there. Small-scale, locally oriented services should be provided — in addition to the large, modern highrises that seem to have become a standard for senior citizens. The boundaries cannot be understood by counting streets, only by knowing the people for whom the services are intended.

The key word is options. A range of alternatives is demanded by the heterogeneity of the elderly population. The ethnic diversity among that group simply adds to the multiplicity of factors to be taken into account in the provision of services. Providing a variety of options allows the elderly

Italian woman who prefers to remain in her neighbourhood to do so. Her sister, who prefers the large complex downtown, can choose this option as well.

That is, a community orientation allows the various characteristics discussed throughout this book to be taken into consideration: numbers and proportion of elderly, family and community support, numbers and proportion of those not speaking English, and of sex, marital status, and cohort differences. A community orientation suggests provincial responsibility in health matters is appropriate, given the need for variation and flexibility in programming. It also allows us to take into account the ethnic types developed earlier from an integration of the various dimensions in the modernization and assimilation processes.

RETURNING TO ETHNIC TYPES

Chapter 2 discussed the major processes of assimilation and modernization, and concluded that for a majority of the elderly in Canada, ethnic assimilation has not taken place. In Chapter 3 the focus was on ethnic identity and pluralism with suggestions that there are important eth-elder types in the many parts of Canada, with different needs that require attention. In Chapter 4, the role of primary-group relations in the life of eth-elders was discussed in regard to care and assistance for the elderly. Preceding sections of this chapter have addressed social policy concerns explicitly. This section now returns to eth-elder types and their needs.

There are at least a half dozen factors such as socioeconomic status, ethnic identity, social segregation, generation Canadian, and degree of urbanization that enter the equation of eth-elder needs. It is difficult to plot and control for all these variations, but several of these polarities can be considered; socioeconomic status and rural-urban polarities have been plotted to provide a starting point (Figure 5.1).

The Jews and the native peoples clearly represent two eth-elder prototypes. Each of these two polar types can be summarized using socioeconomic status and urbanization as differentiating factors, to which a discussion of ethnic identity, social segregation, and generation Canadian can be added. As illustrated in Figure 5.1, the north Europeans and the south Europeans also tend to cluster well; charter eth-elders, the British and the French, also need to be included. Further, policies and service needs may or may not vary by eth-elder type, depending on conditions. Attention is directed here to developing a typology from the range presented earlier.

Urban High Status Type

Jewish eth-elders are the most urban, they are more educated, their average incomes are higher, and their occupational status is higher than any of the others. Recall that 16.5 percent of the Jews are over 65 years of age, a

FIGURE 5.1

ETH-ELDER TYPES BY SOCIOECONOMIC STATUS
AND DEGREE OF URBANIZATION

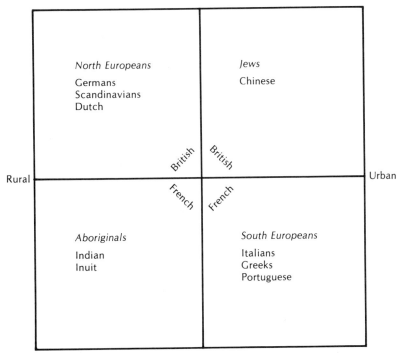

High
Socioeconomic Status

North Europeans
Germans
Scandinavians
Dutch

Jews
Chinese

British British

Rural · Urban

French French

Aboriginals
Indian
Inuit

South Europeans
Italians
Greeks
Portuguese

Low
Socioeconomic Status

greater proportion than any other. They are highly segregated in a few of the main urban centres like Montreal, Toronto, and Winnipeg, and studies show that their ethnic identity is high. Jewish eth-elders represent rising urban "Grey Powers," to the extent that they have resources both to meet their own needs and to lobby for societal changes to meet their needs. In addition, Jewish eth-elders came to Canada in two major waves of immigration, before World War I and after World War II; relatively few came during the inter-war period. They represent pre-holocaust Jews, and holocaust survivors with very different experiences.

The Jewish elderly have modernized but have not assimilated, so that they retain their religious and ethnic identification. They have acculturated and adjusted, however, by entering language, occupational, and educational spheres of the larger society. Indeed, they have integrated to the extent that their influence in the larger society is more considerable than their small numbers might suggest.

Given the urban concentrations of the Jews, together with their economic resources, it is not surprising to see special facilities like Baycrest Centre in Toronto or ethnic personal care homes in other provinces. There are members of this community who are actively involved in programming and policy. Thomas and Wister (1984) suggest that emphasis on socioeconomic achievement within the Jewish cultural tradition often overrides kin obligations that can lead to joint or extended living arrangements. In these circumstances it becomes necessary to ensure the provision of other options preferred by other members of the group. Are adequate services accessible to those who prefer to stay in their own homes or prefer sheltered housing? The diversity of needs even within one ethnic group should still be met.

For Jewish elderly not located in urban centres, the experience of aging will be very different. Indeed, it may be more similar to Europeans living in a multicultural setting or to British elders living as minorities among the French majority in Quebec. It is also important to ask whether knowledgeable persons within the Jewish community assist members of other ethnic groups in meeting the needs of their own members? Are there lessons to be learned from them?

Like the Jewish eth-elder type, Chinese elders are also very urban, they are often segregated in Chinatowns, and their ethnic identity is high. They are also unique because of restrictions on immigration before World War I. As a result, most Chinese eth-elders are single (widowed or bachelors). Thus, the Chinese elderly require housing where ethnic social supports can be provided especially for males. They tend to work in the more modern occupations, but as a group are not as wealthy as the Jews. They have strong kin ties, but there is some evidence (Chan's (1983) study of elderly Chinese women in Montreal) that kin relations are changing. Chinese elders are partially modernized and partially acculturated, showing a different mix than the types discussed thus far.

It has also been shown that the Chinese participate less than Canadians and Europeans in the receipt of government benefits. National census data show that elderly Chinese Canadians are distinctive in that they are more likely to be widowed, and they are more likely to live with others who are not their spouse or children. This suggests that services now provided either to the individual or to the traditional family of the individual may be inappropriate for this group. Non-institutional collective settings require greater attention. What range of accommodation can be provided to maintain and enhance such group settings?

Rural Low Status Type

The needs of aboriginal eth-elders are vastly different than the needs of the Jews. The majority of Canada's Indians and Inuit are segregated in the

Northlands region, and many are of low education, income, and occupational status. Only 3.5 percent have reached the age of 65 or more (their life expectancy is much lower than that of other groups), a relatively small group scattered throughout the Northwest Territories and the northern parts of the six most westerly provinces. They were the first to come to what is now Canada, their ethnic identity is high, and they are greatly dependent on family support for their survival.

The native peoples provide unique policy questions in that the federal government is responsible for aboriginal needs, their small numbers are scattered where it is difficult to reach them, and they are not at all concentrated in one place where institutions can be built to serve their needs. As they were wards of the federal government in the past, this has also unfortunately resulted in less autonomy. Policies have not always met the special needs of Indians and Inuit. First and foremost is the need to develop strategies that will allow native Indians themselves to devise programming that is culturally appropriate. There is also an obvious and immediate need to alter the substandard conditions under which many live. They should be able to contribute in a substantial way to the direction and determination of the types of help they need.

Aboriginals on reserves, as well as those who live in the city, often wish to maintain some of the primary features of their past. Native elderly in particular are characterized by larger informal networks and larger households, with more people around them. Suitable housing should be made available to accommodate such extended family and friendship living patterns. Some studies suggest that aboriginal elderly enjoy higher status and are treated better within their native culture than is true for non-natives. Research is needed to document whether this is accurate.

Furthermore, larger social networks do not necessarily mean that native people require fewer formal services than others. Their health often deteriorates sooner, suggesting they may need more services. However, Indian elders in Winnipeg are less likely to utilize home care services than others. While they are just as likely to utilize physicians' services, medical care may not be the most appropriate service to meet many of their needs. Native Indians have also expressed a strong preference for culturally relevant services in their own language, delivered by members of their own group.

Rural High Status Type

Canada's north European elders, such as German, Dutch, and Scandinavian elders, fall clearly into the higher socioeconomic rural cell of Figure 5.1. Rural prairie eth-elders, many of whom were farmers and have now moved to small hamlets and villages to retire, are of this type. They were pioneers on the prairies. They may not be as well-to-do as Jewish elders, but most are fairly well off. Also, they are usually surrounded by one or more children who still farm or do business in the area, as well as many of their grandchildren and life-long friends. These north European eth-elders are more scattered than Jewish elders, but more accessible than aboriginal elders; they are independent economically; and they are able to continue their friendship and community networks.

They can manage well with a little government assistance, especially in Saskatchewan where they may receive financial assistance to hire help for household chores such as lawn mowing, painting, or cleaning. Government financial supplements to build ethnic or community institutions are a good investment here, because kin and friends can usually manage and run such institutions economically and well. These north European elders may be second generation, whose ancestors came in the 1870s, so they speak both their mother tongue and English well: or they may be first generation, who came to Canada between the wars, and whose English is more tentative. Eth-elders of both generations still prefer to speak their ethnic tongue. Services, therefore, must be rendered in both tongues, because ethnic identity, ethnic mother tongue, and culture are still very important to these elders.

The multicultural and agricultural setting looms large in any consideration of social policy. Access to a pool of resource people from each of the different ethnic groups is an important resource to consider. The rural setting means services exclusive to one group may be inappropriate, unless ethnic bloc settlements exist similar to the ones A. B. Anderson (1972) studied in Saskatchewan. The extent to which older populations in rural towns on the prairies migrate south or elsewhere in the winter months is just beginning to be examined. Most prairie elders were pioneers who survived the depression of the 1930s, so they may still be reluctant to leave the familiar north. This poses interesting questions for the provision of services, which then also require seasonal adjustment.

Urban Low Status Type

South European eth-elders such as the Italians, Greeks and, most recently, Portuguese are for the most part first-generation migrants who came to Canada after World War II. They spent half or more of their lives in the old country, men usually learned English after they were adults at work, and many women who stayed at home had few opportunities to learn English well. Their cultural distinctions are usually very evident. They try to maintain cultural traditions in their homes, and to a large extent are segregated in urban ethnic enclaves. Their education is usually limited (some are illiterate), their occupational status is low, and their incomes are limited. G. Anderson's (1974) Portuguese in Toronto are a good example.

Of the four types discussed so far, these eth-elders are the most dependent on their families when they are old, and their ethnic community usually does not have the means to provide extensive institutions for them. Like the Jews, they can easily be found in larger cities like Montreal, Toronto, and

Vancouver, where services can be provided more easily. But, unlike Jewish elders, they are largely dependent on outside help once family resources have been exhausted. Municipal and provincial government help is crucial.

Visible Minorities

American literature shows that in the United States considerable research has been done on elderly blacks and chicanos, members of visible minorities. Since in Canada visible minorities (blacks, Asians, East Indians, etc.) represent only about 5 percent of the population, they have not been placed in our typological schema. Large numbers have arrived only recently, as a part of the new immigration point system designed in the 1960s. Like the aboriginals, these non-caucasian elderly are only a small proportion of the total minority segment. In many respects, they are more like the south Europeans in that they have come recently. Most of them were born outside Canada, they identify strongly with their cultural background, they prefer to use their mother tongue, and ingroup and family networks are very important to them.

However, visible minorities are unique in that many of the elderly came as refugees and find it very difficult to learn English and adjust to Canadian values and culture. While younger members of their family adjust faster, they often find themselves in conflict with the changing values of their kin. Furthermore, evidence of prejudice and discrimination (Driedger and Mezoff 1981; Driedger and Clifton 1984) shows that the elderly of visible minorities are faced with more discrimination than other ethnic minorities. While there are as yet few elderly among the visible minorities, this will change as more new immigrants arrive, and as those among us age. It is clear that considerable attention will need to be given to services for these minority Canadians. Their needs will, however, be very similar to those of the south Europeans.

French Charter Type

The French and British charter elders have been plotted in a ring in the middle of Figure 5.1 because together they represent two-thirds of the total Canadian population and more than three-fourths of the population aged 65 and over. The French of both rural and urban residence tend to be heavily represented on the lower socioeconomic end, while the British, who are also both rural and urban, tend to locate more toward the upper socioeconomic end. A large majority of the French elders are located in Quebec where they are politically dominant, where their linguistic and cultural way of life has been perpetuated for more than 350 years. Most French elders in Quebec have spent their lives in settings described by Miner (1939) in the village of St. Denis, or more recently in modern villages like Gold's (1975)

St. Pascal. These old rural settings are uniquely French environs. Other elders have moved to the larger cities, but with a familiar French majority culture as is found in Quebec City.

French elders elsewhere in Canada reflect the similarities of the region. Those on the prairies often live in small hamlets like north Europeans do. In northern New Brunswick, they are often segregated into have-not areas like those inhabited by the aboriginals, and in many cities they are also segregated like south Europeans. The province of Quebec has the opportunity to serve their French elder population very well because they are easy to contact in one region. Those who are scattered elsewhere in Canada, however, experience the same problems as other non-charter eth-elders.

British Charter Type

In our figure, the British charter elders have been plotted in the upper half of the socioeconomic scale, and the British elders are heavily located in southern Ontario in the industrial heartland of Canada. Like the Jews, many have lived in cities most of their lives, and they represent the whole range of immigrants. The ancestors of some came generations ago, while others are first generation. In rural southern Ontario, British elders are a majority, although in the metropolitan areas other eth-elder groups are increasing in size at a fast rate. In other parts of the country, British elders, like the French, take on the typical characteristics of the region. They are like north Europeans on the prairie farms, they are like a segregated minority in French Quebec, and in far away, segregated places like rural Newfoundland, British fishermen reflect many traits of aboriginals in the Northlands. As indicated earlier, British eth-elders are perhaps the most diverse of all — hardly a monolithic ethnic majority to which all others assimilate in a uniform way. Outside of Quebec, British elders have a distinct advantage in that English is one of the official languages. However, in many ways their needs are as diverse as the needs of other eth-elders.

Having reviewed the diversity of eth-elder needs, we hope that clustering this diversity into eth-elder types will provide some suggestion for policies. So far it is evident that these needs will vary by socioeconomic status, ethnic identity, generation Canadian, degree of urbanization, and degree of segregation. Further, while education and income may be important for eth-elder status, continuing to be a part of kin networks, remaining in the context of a social community, and receiving services in a familiar ethnic setting may be more important for eth-elder life satisfaction after retirement than occupational status. It is these needs that require further examination for policy considerations.

No mention has been made of the many elderly who claim that they are "Canadian," including many of mixed ethnic ancestry. Hoyt and Babchuk (1981) argue that ethnic identification is a matter of self-selection. Many of mixed ancestry or of low ethnic identification choose to be "Canadian."

However, high ethnic identifiers and visible minorities usually do not have that choice. Chappell (1980) found 23 percent of the elderly living in Winnipeg, not in long-term institutional care, indicated that their ethnicity was Canadian when asked if they considered themselves a member of a particular ethnic group. Fully, 39 percent claimed no ethnic affiliation. How the needs of elders who designate themselves Canadian or of no ethnic identification differ from those claiming ethnic identification has not been investigated sufficiently.

It has been argued throughout that the ethnic context can be critical in the consideration of social policy and service delivery. The basic underlying principles for health care delivery, however, do not differ from one group to another. We turn now to a brief discussion of some of these basic guidelines.

Basic Principles

It is important to recognize that ethnicity is a *potential* factor that may or may not be important, depending on the individual. Even persons who are members of an ethnic group and for whom such identification is important will reflect individual variations. When dealing with services for an individual, rules made for everyone must allow sufficient flexibility for individual differences. Perhaps most important is the need for policies to reflect flexibility and a range of options. That range of options can take ethnicity into account when it is important. Further, the ethnic option must be one that the intended group considers satisfying.

This range of options suggests an acceptance of a broad definition of health, including physical, mental, social, and subjective aspects, together with the interaction of these components with one another. Further, it assumes dynamic, ongoing change in the lives of individuals and in society. Such a broad definition assumes that the significance of disease, especially chronic disease, is measured in terms of the extent to which an individual's ability to function is impaired.

Options within a continuum of care generally include adjustment and integrative services such as pre-retirement and post-retirement counselling, bereavement counselling, specialized recreational programs, and supportive community services. Community services include homemaker, outreach, friendly visiting, and transportation services. These services are designed to assist the elderly to remain living in their usual environment within the community. There are also long-term care facilities for the frail elderly and specialized terminal care facilities and services.

Flexibility within the system implies co-operation, co-ordination, and an interface between formal and informal systems of care. It should be remembered that self-care, not professional care, constitutes the majority of personal health care. Most elderly persons care for themselves on a day-to-day basis and most treat problems themselves before seeking formal services.

Among those who seek formal care, many forms of self-care still continue, and even for specific ailments a combination of personal and formal remedy is frequently utilized (DeFriese and Woomert 1983).

Further, people's ability to care for themselves changes, it is not a stable phenomenon. Changes can be short-term or long-term. Many of these changes are tied to the informal network of which most of us are a part. If an elderly person has an accident, for example, and recovery is short term, it is frequently possible for family and friends to reorganize their schedules to assist the individual on a short-term basis. However, over an extended period of time it is more difficult for the informal network to give time-consuming assistance. In order to be flexible and to respond to changing needs, reassessment has to be a part of the system.

Ingenuity is also demanded. In communities where the ethnic elderly are dispersed or few in number, having those who are available involved may be the most appropriate alternative rather than ethno-cultural services.

For services to be utilized, they must be available and potential clients must be aware of them. It is not only necessary for individuals to know they exist, the services must be accessible. Potential clients must believe that the service can do some good or at minimum do no harm. Fear and mistrust of insensitive agency personnel will not induce individuals to use the service.

Schafer (1985), a philosopher and medical ethicist, suggests two guiding principles in policy making for an aging population. They are equally applicable in the provision of services to the ethnic elderly. First, protect the autonomy of the individual and allow that individual to decide whether he or she wishes to utilize services, the arrangement of services, and the mix of services. Second, where it is deemed absolutely necessary to impose control, use the least restrictive alternative possible. Unless mentally imcompetent (and even where individuals are legally defined incompetent, it does not mean they are imcompetent in all areas), the individual should be provided with appropriate information to make informed decisions.

Throughout this and preceding chapters, there has been an emphasis on unanswered questions, the lack of knowledge, and the need for more research. Many questions have been raised for further research. It is appropriate, therefore, to devote attention to some of the critical methodological issues relevant to future work in this area. In the last section of this chapter we turn to research needs. The discussion is relevant to policy makers and practitioners, not only students and academics, because they should be aware of the types of knowledge necessary in order to make program decisions.

RESEARCH REQUIREMENTS

Research on ethnicity and aging in Canada is growing. It is imperative that *Canadian* research be conducted because the major ethnic groups and their cultural contexts differ considerably from those in the United States, mainly because cultural diversity in Canada is greater. The call for more Canadian research, however, assumes attention to critical methodological issues so as to avoid misinterpretation.

First, several studies of the same phenomenon are required using a variety of different methodologies before one can discuss with confidence the types of ethnic issues that are raised here. Single studies, no matter how good, must be supplemented with studies replicated in a variety of places and situations. No one study can include all relevant factors. Any one study is necessarily restricted in time, place, and the population it encompasses. The Chinese elderly in Vancouver may differ in important ways from the Chinese elderly in Toronto. Studies also vary considerably in the research questions they ask, so that comparability is frequently limited.

It is also important not to generalize beyond the limits permissible, given the constraints of the data. The basic question to ask is not, does assimilation take place from one generation to the next, but rather, in which areas and under what circumstances do pluralism and assimilation take place and in which areas and under what circumstances do they not? If only one area is studied (say parent-child interactions), generalizing to other areas is not acceptable unless the data warrant it. If there are data on physician utilization, generalization to the entire health care system is not appropriate. If there are data on days spent in bed, we must not generalize to all aspects of health.

Comparative data are essential to examine similarities and differences between ethnic groups. If only the Chinese elderly are studied, it is difficult to say anything about these Chinese compared with the French, Japanese, or Jamaicans. Given the current state of research in this area, both quantitative and indepth qualitative studies are required to understand the issues involved. Qualitative studies (participant observation, ethnographies, anthropological approaches) have a special role to play in the study of ethnicity. It is frequently this type of methodology (used singly, prior to, or in conjunction with more quantitative approaches) that informs us whether our words (questions) mean the same thing to members of the different groups being studied and whether the method of inquiry is appropriate. The problem of differences in the meaning of friendships in different subcultures such as blacks, natives, and single-room occupants has already been discussed. Furthermore, the methodology used to study one group may not be appropriate to study another. It may be appropriate and fruitful to study the experience of pain among Italian elders by interviewing; this technique is likely to be less satisfactory among the Japanese, who consider expression of pain or suffering a sign of weakness (Ujimoto 1986).

Research designs must also include a multiplicity of factors. A recurrent theme in the literature is a conceptual distinction between ethnic cultural factors and structural factors such as class and racial prejudice (Ujimoto

1983). The importance of the class variable was raised in the second chapter. As Jansen and Mueller (1983) point out, the general literature on age stratification suggests the continuity of the stratification process from middle to old age. Atchley and associates (1979), while not studying ethnic groups, underscore the need to incorporate measures of social stratification in studies of families in later life. Class and racial prejudice seriously influence the individual's life, but are not related in a linear fashion to modernization or assimilation. With the Jewish elderly, high socioeconomic status and high ethnic identity co-exist. However, native Indians have low socioeconomic status, suffer from discrimination and prejudice, and also demonstrate high ethnic identity.

The study of the elderly in general requires both longitudinal and cross-sectional data. Botwinick (1983) indicates that one of the major difficulties facing researchers in aging is the problem of disentangling age, cohort, and period (time of measurement effects). This separation of potential causes is necessary to understand age (or maturational) processes as distinct from environmental factors. The effects of period or time of measurement include situational factors influencing assessment at different times (the respondent could be sick at time$_1$ but not time$_2$, etc.). Cohorts of people born in the same time-interval who age together (Riley 1976, 194) experience similar historical events and their consequences (Bengtson and Cutler 1976). That is, different age groups have been affected by, and share, the historical events they have experienced.

An example illustrates the importance of disentangling these effects in gerontology. Elderly persons as a group have worse hearing than younger adults. Is this due to physiological changes as they age or is it due to exposure to high levels of noise throughout their lives? To know the answer, longitudinal data are required, including different cohorts of elderly persons, some having been exposed to high noise levels in their occupation (e.g., a riveter) throughout their lives, and some not (e.g., a librarian).

Age versus cohort effects are aptly demonstrated in Botwinick's example (borrowed from Kastenbaum), where a researcher occasionally chats with elderly people in a certain community and observes that they all speak with an Italian accent. In chatting with the younger people, it is obvious they do not speak with such an accent. Conclusion: as people grow older they develop Italian accents, that is, an age effect. The point is, of course, that such differences reflect cultural backgrounds, not the aging process. They reflect cohort differences.

The importance of distinguishing between cohort and age differences is illustrated when Botwinick changes the example. In chatting with younger and older residents of the community, the researcher observes many of the elderly are not as quick in their behaviours, their reaction times are slower than for the younger people. The conclusion, frequently made, is that a prime age effect is a slowing down. There are methods (none of which are fail proof) for disentangling age and cohort effects. They include what are known as cross-sequential designs, which incorporate both longitudinal and cross-sectional data, analyzed and compared in specific ways. However, this is an expensive and time-consuming strategy, seldom employed in research but nevertheless necessary.

The issue of age versus cohort effects is similar to disentangling age and generational differences among members of an ethnic group. Are observed differences between older and younger Ukrainians due to age or to the generational (cohort) differences in their experiences? Such questions show the need for collection of more sociohistorical data about the current cohort of elderly persons. Longitudinal data would be needed to complement cross-sectional studies.

Where longitudinal data are not available, some authors study members of different generations within cross-sectional designs. Studying members of different generations at one point in time, Osako (1979) in the United States, and Sugiman and Nishio (1983) in Canada, both conclude that Japanese immigrants demonstrate generational differences with a widening intergenerational status gap as the younger generation moves up socially and economically. Both conclude that there is an emphasis within the Japanese family on its corporateness rather than on individualism. Nevertheless, future generations of Japanese elders in North America will probably not rely on younger members to any great extent during their old age. Similarly, Wu (1975) argues that Chinese Americans have become assimilated in such a way that filial piety no longer holds the place that it once did.

Evaluation Research and Needs Assessments

Policy makers and practitioners are frequently interested in evaluation research. Indeed, there has been a great increase in the popularity of this type of research in recent years. There are two kinds of evaluation research. One is known as outcome (summative) evaluations of the effectiveness of a particular program. Does adult day care prevent or postpone hospitalization and long-term institutionalization? Does the provision of community support to elderly individuals increase their quality of life? In each instance interest is focused on assessing the program to evaluate whether its impact is feasible or appropriate. Evaluations can also be process oriented (formative), where the emphasis is on the process of what is happening in the system to improve that system.

There tends to be an emphasis on summative rather than formative evaluation. This is partly due to a misunderstanding of the value of the research process. It is, for one thing, very difficult to conduct rigorous evaluations within the real world (that is, out of the laboratory) because not all relevant factors can be controlled. Furthermore, leaders of organizations tend to ask global questions, such as: Is this program worthwhile? Such questions are difficult to answer without large amounts of research money and much time spent in research. The conduct of outcome evaluations also tends to threaten staff, since the results could be negative.

In most instances it is more appropriate to view evaluations as a strategy for increasing knowledge to improve the system. Research tends not to be presented in such a nonthreatening context. It is, however, more realistic and usually more useful to conduct process evaluations, particularly when outsiders collaborate well with insiders. The strengths of each can combine to fill gaps in knowledge and improve the operation of the system. This requires a recognition that one research project will not provide the answers to all questions; perhaps it will not provide a definitive answer to even one question.

Policy makers are also frequently interested in needs assessments. Needs assessments differ from evaluations in that they are conducted to identify the needs of a particular target population. Needs assessments can take many forms, including face-to-face interviews, with prospective users of a service, town hall or community forums, interviewing key informants, or using available data from the census or other sources. A major difficulty with needs assessments is knowing what needs we want to assess and how these needs can be measured.

Another major difficulty is that often people do not know how their needs can best be met without knowing the various alternatives. This is reflected in studies where respondents are asked what services or what facilities they would like. Often they reply none or that they do not know. This is especially a problem if such answers are interpreted as lack of need when in fact they reflect a lack of knowledge about the alternatives. Interpretations that assume respondents do not know what they want, however, enable practitioners or policy makers rather than potential clients to make decisions on future services. For example, in a study of housing for Canadian Indians, it may be better to document the characteristics of existing accommodation (such as whether there is running water, hot water, heating, etc.) using standard guidelines, rather than ask Indians themselves for the type of accommodation they would like to live in. If they know only substandard housing or think that is the only option, how can they be expected to know details about better housing or to prefer a higher standard? On the other hand, whose standard should be used — the client's or the service provider's?

It is also worth mentioning that other types of research that are not generally classified as research evaluations or as needs assessments offer much valuable information. These studies can include survey research, ethnographic studies, and reviews of the literature and an integration of existing knowledge. Research does not have to be evaluation research or needs assessments to be relevant for policy makers and practitioners.

CONCLUSIONS

In this chapter some of the policy implications for the delivery of services to eth-elders have been examined. It has been emphasized that ethnicity is an important factor but that it may not be relevant for everyone. The recognition that ethnicity is potentially important suggests that services should be based on need rather than age (while maintaining universality and accessibility). Several policy concerns for meeting the needs of eth-elders have been discussed.

When ethnic traditions are strong, one of the best means for ensuring adequate and appropriate services is control of services by the ethnic group itself. In this situation cultural congruence is more likely to take place. Continuity is an important feature of life satisfaction during old age — an important feature for all ages. Cultural change from rural to urban environments for eth-elders today must be especially attended to so as to retain continuity between familiar relatives, friends, spatial arrangements, and the like. Many of the recommendations found in the literature dealing with ethnic elders are similar to the suggestions reported in the gerontological literature in general. All of us like familiar surroundings. Continuity with past lifestyles and environments helps assure that our needs and preferences have been taken into account.

Particular attention has been paid to the importance of the delivery of services within a familiar community context. Such a community need not include spatial proximity, but can be defined by social networks instead. Community, in its sociological sense, encompasses the important features of a person's life, which we argue must be taken into account in the delivery of services. To work at the community level, one must know the individual and his or her needs.

We also propose that ethnic types exist and that policies and services for these eth-elder types vary enormously. More research is required to examine the extent of these similarities and differences. One of the main points is that a service delivery system to meet the needs of all elders, including the needs of eth-elders, will require: (1) a continuum of care with a range of options, (2) services that fall within a broad definition of health, (3) services that are co-ordinated and flexible, and (4) services where the autonomy of the individual recipient of care is protected whenever possible. Finally, some basic research requirements were discussed. There is a great need for more knowledge.

The challenge to lay people, policy makers, practitioners, and researchers alike is to pay greater attention to the heterogeneous community of elderly persons who have salient ethnic life experiences. Together with eth-elders we can learn of their rich histories, varying circumstances, and unique needs. In the process we will all gain in shared knowledge.

BIBLIOGRAPHY

Abu-Laban, S.
1980   "The Family Life of Older Canadians." Pp. 125–34 in V. W. Marshall
       (ed.), *Aging in Canada: Social Perspectives*. Don Mills, Ontario: Fitz-
       henry & Whiteside.
Abu-Laban, S., and B. Abu-Laban
1980   "Women and the Aged as Minority Groups: A Critique." Pp. 63–79 in
       V. W. Marshall (ed.), *Aging in Canada: Social Perspectives*. Don Mills,
       Ontario: Fitzhenry & Whiteside.
Adams, J. P.
1980   "Service Arrangements Preferred by Minority Elderly: A Cross-cultural
       Survey." *Journal of Gerontological Social Work* 3:39–57.
Amenson, C. S., and P. M. Lewinshon
1981   "An Investigation into the Observed Sex Differences in Prevalence of
       Unipolar Depression." *Journal of Abnormal Psychology* 90:1–13.
Anderson, A. B.
1972   "Assimilation in the Bloc Settlements of North-Central Saskatchewan:
       A Comparative Study of Identity Change among Seven Ethno-Religious
       Groups in a Canadian Prairie Region." Ph.D. dissertation, University of
       Saskatchewan.
Anderson, G.
1974   *Networks of Contact: The Portuguese and Toronto*. Waterloo, On-
       tario: Wilfred Laurier University Press.
Atchley, R. C.
1972   *The Social Forces in Later Life*. California: Wadsworth.
Atchley, R. C., L. Pignatello, and E. C. Shaw
1979   "Interactions with Family and Friends: Marital Status and Occupational
       Differences among Older Women." *Research on Aging* 1:83–96.
Austin, C. D., and M. B. Loeb
1982   "Why Age Is Relevant in Social Policy and Practice." Pp. 263–88 in
       B. L. Neugarten (ed.), *Age or Need? Public Policies for Older People*.
       Beverly Hills, California: Sage Publications.
Barnes, G. E., and N. L. Chappell
1982   "Old but Not Depressed." Papers presented at the annual meeting of
       the Canadian Association of Gerontology, Winnipeg, Manitoba,
       November.
Barron, M.
1953   "Minority Group Characteristics of the Aged in American Society."
       Journal of Gerontology 8:477–82.

1954   "Attacking Prejudices against the Aged." Pp. 56–58 in *Growing with the Years*, Legislative Document No. 32. New York: New York Legislative Committee on Problems of Aging.

1961   *The Aging American*. New York: Crowell.

Bastida, E. M.

1983   "Minority Decision-Making, Accessibility, and Resource Utilization in the Provision of Services: Urban-Rural Differences." Pp. 212–25 in R. L. McNeely and J. L. Colen (eds.), *Aging in Minority Groups*. Beverly Hills, California: Sage Publications.

Beattie, W. M.

1976   "Aging and the Social Services." Pp. 619–42 in R. H. Binstock and E. Shanas (eds.), *Handbook of Aging and the Social Sciences*. New York: Van Nostrand Reinhold.

Begin, M.

1982   *Canadian Government Report on Aging*. Ottawa: Department of National Health and Welfare, June.

Bengtson, V. L., and N. L. Cutler

1976   "Generational and Intergenerational Relations: Perspectives on Age Groups and Social Change." Pp. 130–59 in R. H. Binstock and E. Shanas (eds.), *Handbook of Aging and the Social Sciences*. New York: Van Nostrand Reinhold.

Bengtson, V. L., J. J. Dowd, D. H. Smith, and A. Inkeles

1975   "Modernization, Modernity, and Perceptions of Aging: A Cross-Cultural Study." *Journal of Gerontology* 30:688–95.

Berger, P. L.

1982   "Secular Branches, Religious Roots." *Society* 20:64–66.

Berk, M. L., and A. B. Bernstein

1982   "Regular Source of Care and the Minority Aged." *Journal of the American Geriatrics Society* 30:251–54.

Biegel, D., and W. Sherman

1979   "Neighbourhood Capacity Building and the Ethnic Aged." Pp. 320–40 in D. Gelfand and A. Kutzik (eds.), *Ethnicity and Aging*. New York: Springer.

Bienvenue, R. M., and B. Havens

1986   "Colonialism and the Lives of the Elderly: A Comparison of Canadian Indian and Non-Indian Communities." Unpublished paper, University of Manitoba.

Blau, Z. S., G. T. Oser, and R. C. Stephens

1979   "Aging, Social Class, and Ethnicity." *Pacific Sociological Review* 22:501–25.

Block, M.

1979   "Exiled Americans: The Plight of Indian Aged in the United States." Pp. 184–92 in D. E. Gelfand and A. J. Kutzik (eds.), *Ethnicity and Aging: Theory, Research, and Policy*. New York: Springer.

Botwinick, J.

1983   "Method and Madness in Aging Research." Pp. 1–65 in N. Chappell (ed.), *Longitudinal Design and Data Analysis in Aging*. Winnipeg: Centre on Aging, University of Manitoba.

Branch, L. G.
    1980   *Vulnerable Elders*, No. 6, Gerontological Monographs. Washington, DC: Gerontological Society of America.
Branch, L. G., and A. M. Jette
    1981   "Elders' Use of Informal Long-Term Care Assistance." Paper presented at the annual meeting of the Gerontological Society of America, Toronto, Ontario.
Breen, L. Z.
    1960   "The Aging Individual." Pp. 145–162 in C. Tibbits (ed.), *Handbook of Social Gerontology*. Chicago: University of Chicago Press.
Breton, R.
    1984   "The Production and Allocation of Symbolic Resources: An Analysis of the Linguistic and Ethnocultural Fields in Canada." *Canadian Review of Sociology and Anthropology* 21:123–44.
Brody, E. M.
    1981   "Women in the Middle and Family Help to Older People." *The Gerontologist* 21:470–80.
Burshtyn, H., and D. G. Smith
    1978   "Occupational Prestige Ratings among High School Students in the Canadian Arctic." Pp. 249–73 in L. Driedger (ed.), *The Canadian Ethnic Mosaic: A Quest for Identity*. Toronto: McClelland and Stewart.
Cantor, M. H.
    1979   "The Informal Support System of New York's Inner City Elderly: Is Ethnicity a Factor?" Pp. 153–73 in D. Gelfand (ed.), *Ethnicity and Aging: Theory, Research and Policy*. New York: Springer.
Carp, F. M.
    1979   "Improving the Functional Quality of Housing and Environments for the Elderly through Transportation." In T. O. Byerts, S. C. Howell and L. A. Pastalan (eds.), *Environmental Context of Aging*. New York: Garland Publishing.
Chan, F. M.
    1983   "Coping with Aging and Managing Self-Identity: The Social World of the Elderly Chinese Women." *Canadian Ethnic Studies* 15:36–50.
Chappell, N. L.
    1980   *Peer and Intergenerational Relations Study*. Study conducted through the Centre on Aging, University of Manitoba, Winnipeg.
    1983   "Informal Support Networks among the Elderly." *Research on Aging* 5:77–99.
    1985   "Social Support and the Receipt of Home Care Services." *The Gerontologist* 25:47–54.
Chappell, N. L., and B. Havens
    1980   "Old and Female: Testing the Double Jeopardy Hypothesis." *Sociological Quarterly* 21:157–71.
    1985   "Who Helps the Elderly Person: A Discussion of Informal and Formal Care." Pp. 211–27 in W. Peterson and J. Quadagno (eds.), *Social Bonds in Later Life*. Beverly Hills, California: Sage Publications.
Chappell, N. L., and M. J. Penning
    1984   "Informal Social Supports: Examining Ethnic Variations." Paper pre-

sented at the annual meeting of the Gerontological Society of America, San Antonio, Texas.

Chappell, N. L., and L. A. Strain
1984 *Needs Assessment of Natives 50+ Living in Winnipeg.* Study conducted through the Centre on Aging, University of Manitoba, Winnipeg.

Chappell, N. L., L. A., Strain, and A. A. Blandford
1986 *Aging and Health Care: A Social Perspective.* Toronto: Holt, Rinehart and Winston.

Cohen, C. I., and H. Rajkowski
1982 "What's in a Friend: Substantive and Theoretical Issues." *The Gerontologist* 22:261–66.

Cohler, B. J.
1979 "Stress or Support: Relations between Older Women from Three European Ethnic Groups and Their Relatives." Pp. 115–20 in D. E. Gelfand and A. J. Kutzik (eds.), *Ethnicity and Aging.* New York: Springer.

Cohler, B., and H. Grunenbaum
1981 *Mothers, Grandmothers, and Daughters.* New York: John Wiley and Sons.

Colen, J. N., and R. L. McNeely
1983 "Minority Aging and Knowledge in the Social Professions: Overview of a Problem." Pp. 15–23 in R. L. McNeely and J. N. Colen (eds.), *Aging in Minority Groups.* Beverly Hills, California: Sage Publications.

Cool, L. E.
1981 "Ethnic Identity: A Source of Community Esteem for the Elderly." *Anthropological Quarterly* 54:179–81.

Coser, L.
1956 *The Functions of Social Conflict.* New York: Free Press.

Coward, R. T.
1979 "Planning Community Services for the Rural Elderly: Implications from Research." *The Gerontologist* 19:275–82.

Cowgill, D. O.
1974 "Aging and Modernization: A Revision of the Theory." Pp. 123–46 in J. F. Gubrium (ed.), *Late Life: Communities and Environmental Policy.* Springfield, Illinois: Charles C. Thomas.

Cowgill, D. O., and L. D. Holmes (eds.)
1972 *Aging and Modernization.* New York: Appleton-Century Crofts.

Creecy, R. F., and R. Wright
1979 "Morale and Informal Activity with Friends among Black and White Elderly." *The Gerontologist* 19:544–47.

Cuellar, I.
1981 "Service Delivery and Mental Health Services for Chicano Elders." Pp. 185–211 in M. Miranda (ed.), *Chicano Aging and Mental Health.* Washington, DC: DHHS Publication #(ADM) 81–952.

Cumming, E.
1964 "New Thoughts on the Theory of Disengagement." Pp. 3–19 in R. Kastenbaum (ed.), *New Thoughts on Old Age.* New York: Springer Publishing.

Cumming, E., L. Dean, D. Hewell, and I. McCaffrey
1960 "Disengagement — A Tentative Theory of Aging." *Sociometry* 23:23–35.
Cumming, E., and L. D. Henry
1961 *Growing Old: The Process of Disengagement*. New York: Basic Books.
Darroch, A. G.
1979 "Another Look at Ethnicity, Stratification and Social Mobility in Canada." *Canadian Journal of Sociology* 4:1–25.
DeFriese, G. H., and A. Woomert
1983 "Self-care among U.S. Elderly: Recent Developments." *Research on Aging* 5:3–23.
deVries, J., and F. G. Vallee
1980 *Language Use in Canada*. Ottawa: Minister of Supply and Services.
Disman, M.
1984 "Explorations in Ethnic Identity, Oldness, and Continuity." Paper presented at the annual meetings of the Gerontological Society of America, San Antonio, Texas.
Dowd, J. J.
1980 "Aging as Exchange: A Preface to Theory." Pp. 103–21 in J. S. Quadagno (ed.), *Aging, the Individual and Society: Readings in Social Gerontology*. New York: St. Martin's Press.
Dowd, J. J., and V. L. Bengtson
1978 "Aging in Minority Populations: An Examination of the Double Jeopardy Hypothesis." *Journal of Gerontology* 33:427–36.
Driedger, L.
1975 "In Search of Cultural Identity Factors: A Comparison of Ethnic Minority Students in Canada." *Canadian Review of Sociology and Anthropology* 12:150–62.
1980 "Nomos-Building on the Prairies: Construction of Indian, Hutterite and Jewish Sacred Canopies." *Canadian Journal of Sociology* 5:341–56.
1985 "Conformity vs. Pluralism: Minority Identities and Inequalities." Pp. 157–74 in N. Nevitte and A. Kornberg (eds.), *Minorities and the Canadian State*. New York: Mosaic Press.
Driedger, L., and G. Church
1974 "Residential Segregation and Institutional Completeness: A Comparison of Ethnic Minorities." *Canadian Review of Sociology and Anthropology* 11:30–52.
Driedger, L., and R. A. Clifton
1984 "Ethnic Stereotypes: Images of Ethnocentrism, Reciprocity or Dissimilarity?" *Canadian Review of Sociology and Anthropology* 21:287–301.
Driedger, L., and R. A. Mezoff
1981 "Ethnic Prejudice and Discrimination in Winnipeg High Schools." *Canadian Journal of Sociology* 6:1–17.
Edwards, E. D.
1983 "Native-American Elders: Current Issues and Social Policy Implications." Pp. 74–82 in R. L. McNeely and J. L. Colen (eds.), *Aging in Minority Groups*. Beverly Hills, California: Sage Publications.

Eisdorfer, C., and D. Cohen
1982 *Mental Health Care of the Aging: A Multidisciplinary Curriculum for Professional Training*. New York: Springer.

Evans, R. G.
1984 *Strained Mercy: The Economics of Canadian Health Care*. Toronto: Butterworths.

Fandetti, D. V., and D. E. Gelfand
1976 "Care of the Aged: Attitudes of White Ethnic Families." *The Gerontologist* 16:544–49.

Fischer, D. H.
1978 *Growing Old in America*. New York: Oxford University Press.

Frideres, J. S.
1983 *Native People in Canada: Contemporary Conflicts* (2nd ed.). Scarborough, Ontario: Prentice-Hall.

Fry, C. L.
1980 *Aging in Culture and Society*. Brooklyn, New York: J. F. Bergin.

Gelfand, D. E.
1982 *Aging: The Ethnic Factor*. Boston: Little, Brown and Company.

Gelfand, D. E., and D. V. Fandetti
1980 "Suburban and Urban White Ethnics: Attitudes toward Care of the Aged." *The Gerontologist* 20:588–94.

Gelfand, D. E., and A. J. Kutzik
1979 *Ethnicity and Aging: Theory, Research and Policy*. New York: Springer.

Gerber, L. M.
1983 "Ethnicity Still Matters: Socio-demographic Profiles of the Ethnic Elderly in Ontario." *Canadian Ethnic Studies* 15:60–80.

Glazer, N., and D. P. Moynihan
1963 *Beyond the Melting Pot*. Cambridge, Massachusetts: M.I.T. Press.

Gold, G. L.
1975 *St. Pascal*. Toronto: Holt, Rinehart and Winston.

Goldstein, M. C., and C. M. Beall
1981 "Modernization and Aging in the Third and Fourth World: Views from the Hinterland in Nepal." *Human Organization* 40:48–55.

Gordon, M.
1964 *Assimilation as a Way of Life*. New York: Oxford University Press.

Grebler, L., J. W. Moore, and R. C. Guzman
1970 *The Mexican American People*. New York: Free Press.

Greene, V. L., and D. J. Monahan
1984 "Comparative Utilization of Community Based Long Term Care Services by Hispanic and Anglo Elderly in a Case Management System." *Journal of Gerontology* 39:730–35.

Gubrium, J. F.
1973 *The Myth of the Golden Years: A Socio-Environmental Theory of Aging*. Springfield, Illinois: Charles C. Thomas.

Guemple, L.
1980 "Growing Old in Inuit Society." Pp. 95–101 in V. W. Marshall (ed.), *Aging in Canada: Social Perspectives*. Don Mills, Ontario: Fitzhenry and Whiteside.

Guttmann, D.
    1973   "Leisure-Time Activity Interests of Jewish Aged." *The Gerontologist* 13:219–23.
    1979   "Use of Informal and Formal Supports by White Ethnic Aged." Pp. 246–62 in D. E. Gelfand and A. J. Kutzik (eds.), *Ethnicity and Aging: Theory, Research and Policy*. New York: Springer.

Hanson, S. L., W. J. Sauer, and W. C. Seelbach
    1983   "Racial and Cohort Variations in Filial Responsibility Norms." *The Gerontologist* 23:626–31.

Hassan, A. H., K. M. Kuldip, and W. C. Nung
    1978   "Ethnic Differences in Mortality from Ischemic Heart Disease: A Study of Migrant and Native Populations." *Journal of Chronic Diseases* 31:137–46.

Hauser, P. M.
    1976   "Aging and World-wide Population Change." Pp. 58–86 in R. H. Binstock and E. Shanas (eds.), *Handbook of Aging and the Social Sciences*. New York: Van Nostrand Reinhold.

Havens, B., and E. Thompson
    1975   "Research Results: Ethnic Variations in Needs of the Elderly." Unpublished paper presented to the Canadian Association on Gerontology, Toronto.

Havighurst, R. J., and R. Albrecht
    1953   *Older People*. New York: Longmans Green

Havighurst, R. J., B. L. Neugarten, and S. S. Tobin
    1968   "Disengagement and Patterns of Aging." Pp. 161–72 in B. L. Neugarten (ed.), *Middle Age and Aging*. Chicago: University of Chicago Press.

Health and Welfare Canada
    1981   *Survey of Old Age Security (O.A.S.) and Canada Pension Plan (C.P.P.) Retirement Benefit Recipients*. Ottawa: Minister of Supply and Services.
    1984   *Expression: Newsletter of the National Advisory Council on Aging*. Ottawa: Health and Welfare Canada.

Health and Welfare Canada and Statistics Canada
    1981   *Canada Health Survey*. Ottawa: Minister of Supply and Services.

Helle, H. J.
    1985   "The Purpose of Max Weber's Sociology: Comments on Steven Seidman ..." *Canadian Journal of Sociology* 10:195–201.

Heltsley, M. E., and R. C. Powers
    1975   "Social Interaction and Perceived Adequacy of Interaction of the Rural Aged." *The Gerontologist* 15:533–36.

Hendricks, J., and C. D. Hendricks
    1977   *Aging in Mass Society: Myths and Realities*. Cambridge, Massachusetts: Winthrop.

Henry, F.
    1973   *Forgotten Canadians: The Blacks of Nova Scotia*. Don Mills, Ontario: Longman Canada

Hirshfeld, R. M., and D. K. Cross
    1982   "Epidemiology of Affective Disorders: Psychosocial Risk Factors." *Archives of General Psychiatry* 39:35–46.

Hochschild, A. R.
1973   *The Unexpected Community*. Englewood Cliffs, New Jersey: Prentice-Hall.

Holzberg, C. S.
1981   "Cultural Gerontology: Towards an Understanding of Ethnicity and Aging." *Culture* 1:110–22.

Homans, G. C.
1961   *Social Behaviour: Its Elementary Forms*. New York: Harcourt.

Horowitz, I. L.
1982   "The New Fundamentalism." *Society* 20:40–47.

Hostetler, J. A., and G. Huntington
1967   *The Hutterites in North America*. New York: Holt, Rinehart and Winston.

Hoyt, D. R., and N. Babchuk
1981   "Ethnicity and the Voluntary Association of the Aged." *Ethnicity* 8:67–81.

Hughes, E. C.
1943   *French Canada in Transition*. Chicago: University of Chicago Press.
1950   "Preface." In *Robert Ezra Park, Race and Culture*. New York: Free Press.

Hughes, E. C., and H. M. Hughes
1952   *Where Peoples Meet*. Glencoe, Illinois: Free Press.

Hum, D., and E. Chan
1980   "Do Minorities Participate in Canada's Old Age Security Programs? A Case Study of the Chinese." Winnipeg: University of Manitoba, Department of Economics, No. 198004.

Isajiw, W. W., and L. Driedger
1986   "Ethnic Identity: Resource or Drawback for Social Mobility?" Unpublished research paper, University of Manitoba.

Isajiw, W. W., and T. Makabe
1982   "Socialization as a Factor in Ethnic Identity Retention." Research Paper No. 134, Centre for Urban and Community Studies, University of Toronto.

Jackson, J. D.
1975   *Community and Conflict: A Study of French/English Relations in Ontario*. Toronto: Holt, Rinehart and Winston.

Jackson, J. J.
1972   "Comparative Life Styles of Family and Friend Relationships among Older Black Women." *Family Coordinator* 21:477–85.

Jansen, P., and K. F. Mueller
1983   "Age, Ethnicity, and Well-Being: A Comparative Study of Anglos, Blacks, and Mexican Americans." *Research on Aging* 5:353–67.

Jarvis, G. K.
1972   "Canadian Old People as a Deviant Minority." Pp. 605–27 in C. L. Boydell, C. E. Grindstaff and P. C. Whitehead (eds.), *Deviant Behaviour and Societal Reaction*. Toronto: Holt, Rinehart and Winston.

John, R.
1985   "Service Needs and Support Networks of Elderly Native Americans: Family, Friends, and Social Service Agencies." Pp. 229–47 in W. A.

Peterson and J. Quadagno (eds.), *Social Bonds in Later Life*. Beverly Hills, California: Sage Publications.

Joy, R. J.
1972 *Languages in Conflict*. Toronto: McClelland and Stewart.

Kahana, E., and B. J. Felton
1977 "Social Context and Personal Need: A Study of Polish and Jewish Aged." *Journal of Social Issues* 33:56–74.

Kalbach, W. E.
1980 *Historical and Generational Perspectives of Ethnic Residential Segregation in Toronto, Canada, 1851–1971*. Toronto: Centre for Urban and Community Studies, University of Toronto.

Kalbach, W. E., and W. W. McVey
1979 *The Demographic Bases of Canadian Society* (2nd ed.). Toronto: McGraw-Hill.

Kalish, R. A., and S. Yuen
1971 "Americans of East-Asian Ancestry: Aging and the Aged." *The Gerontologist* 11:36–47.

Kallen, H.M.
1924 *Culture and Democracy in the United States*. New York: Liveright.

Kammerman, S. B.
1976 "Community Services for the Aged: The View from Eight Countries." *The Gerontologist* 16:529–37.

Kaplan, M.
1979 *Leisure: Lifestyle and Lifespan: Perspectives for Gerontology*. Philadelphia: W. B. Saunders.

Keith, J.
1980 "Old Age and Community Creation." Pp. 170–97 in C. L. Fry (ed.), *Aging in Culture and Society*. Brooklyn, New York: J. F. Bergin.

Kelly, M.
1983 "The Aging of Canada's Native Population." A poster session presented at the 12th annual scientific and educational meeting of the Canadian Association on Gerontology, Moncton, New Brunswick, October.

Kim, P. K. H.
1983 "Demography of the Asian-Pacific Elderly: Selected Problems and Implications." Pp. 29–41 in R. L. McNeely and J. L. Colen (eds.), *Aging in Minority Groups*. Beverly Hills, California: Sage Publications.

Krickus, M. A.
1980 "The Status of East European Women in the Family: Tradition and Change." Pp. 76–96 in *Conference on the Educational and Occupational Needs of White Ethnic Women*. Washington, DC: National Institute of Education.

Kutza, E. A., and N. R. Zweibel
1982 "Age as a Criterion for Focusing Public Programs." Pp. 55–99 in B. L. Neugarten (ed.), *Age or Need? Public Policies for Older People*. Beverly Hills, California: Sage Publications.

Kuypers, J. A., and V. L. Bengtson
1973 "Social Breakdown and Competence: A Model of Normal Aging." *Human Development* 16:181–201.

Laslett, P.
  1976   "Societal Development and Aging." Pp. 87–116 in R. Binstock and E.
          Shanas (eds.), *Handbook of Aging and the Social Sciences*. New York:
          Van Nostrand Reinhold.
Lieberson, S.
  1970   *Language and Ethnic Relations in Canada*. Toronto: Wiley.
Lin, N.
  1982   "Social Resources and Instrumental Action." Pp. 131–45 in P. V. Mars-
          den and N. Lin (eds.), *Social Structure and Network Analysis*. Beverly
          Hills, California: Sage Publications.
Linn, M. W., K. I. Hunter, and P. R. Perry
  1979   "Differences by Sex and Ethnicity in the Psychosocial Adjustment of the
          Elderly." *Journal of Health and Social Behavior* 20:273–81.
Lipman, A.
  1982   "Minority Aging from the Exchange and Structuralist-Functionalist Per-
          spectives." Pp. 195–202 in R. C. Manuel (ed.), *Minority Aging: Socio-
          logical and Social Psychological Issues*. Westport, Connecticut: Green-
          wood Press.
Lum, D.
  1983   "Asian-Americans and Their Aged." Pp. 85–94 in R. L. McNeely and
          J. L. Colen (eds.), *Aging in Minority Groups*. Beverly Hills, California:
          Sage Publications.
MacLean, M. J., and R. Bonar
  1983   "The Ethnic Elderly in a Dominant Culture Long-Term Care Facility."
          Canadian Ethnic Studies 15:51–59.
Maddox, G. L.
  1968   "Persistence of Life Style among the Elderly: A Longitudinal Study of
          Patterns of Social Activity in Relation to Life Satisfaction." Pp. 181–83
          in B. L. Neugarten (ed.), *Middle Age and Aging*. Chicago: University of
          Chicago Press.
Manuel, R. C. (ed.)
  1982   *Minority Aging: Sociological and Social Psychological Issues*. West-
          port, Connecticut: Greenwood Press.
Markides, K. S.
  1983   "Minority Aging." Pp. 115–38 in M. W. Riley, B. B. Hess and K. Bond
          (eds.), *Aging in Society: Reviews of Recent Literature*. Hillsdale, New
          Jersey: Lawrence Erlbaum.
Markides, K. S., J. S. Boldt, and L. A. Ray
  1986   "Sources of Helping and Intergenerational Solidarity, Findings from a
          Three-Generations Study." *Journal of Gerontology* July, forthcoming.
Markides, K. S., D. S. Costley, and L. Rodriguez
  1981   "Perceptions of Intergenerational Relations and Psychological Well-
          being among Elderly Mexican Americans: A Causal Model." *Interna-
          tional Journal of Aging and Human Development* 13:43–52.
Martinez, M. Z.
  1979   "Los Ancianos: Attitudes of Mexican Americans Regarding Family Sup-
          port of the Elderly." Ph.D. dissertation, Florence Heller Graduate
          School for Advanced Studies in Social Welfare, Brandeis University.

Matthiasson, J. S., and C. J. Matthiasson
1978 "A People Apart: The Ethnicization of the Inuit of the Eastern Canadian Arctic." Pp. 235–48 in L. Driedger (ed.), *The Canadian Ethnic Mosaic*. Toronto: McClelland and Stewart.

McKinlay, J. B.
1973 "Social Networks, Lay Consultation and Help-Seeking Behavior." *Social Forces* 51:275–92.

Mindel, C. H., and R. Wright
1982 "The Use of Social Services by Black and White Elderly: The Role of Social Support Systems." *Journal of Gerontological Social Work* 4:107–20.

Miner, H.
1939 *St. Denis: A French-Canadian Parish*. Chicago: University of Chicago Press.

Mitchell, J., and J. C. Register
1984 "An Exploration of Family Interaction with the Elderly by Race, Socio-economic Status, and Residence." *The Gerontologist* 24:48–54.

Morrison, B. J.
1983 "Sociocultural Dimensions: Nursing Homes and the Minority Aged." Pp. 127–45 in G. S. Getzel and M. J. Mellor (eds.), *Gerontological Social Work Practice in Long-term Care*. New York: The Haworth Press.

Mossey, J. M., B. Havens, N. P. Roos, and E. Shapiro
1981 "The Manitoba Longitudinal Study on Aging: Description and Methods." *The Gerontologist* 21:551–58.

Myers, G. C.
1982 "Cross-national Variations in Family Structures among the Aged." Paper presented at the annual meeting of the Gerontological Society of America, Boston, Massachusetts.

Neugarten, B. L.
1982a "Older People: A Profile." Pp. 33–54 in B. L. Neugarten (ed.), *Age or Need? Public Policies for Older People*. Beverly Hills, California: Sage Publications.
1982b "Policy for the 1980's: Age or Need Entitlement?" Pp. 19–32 in B. L. Neugarten (ed.), *Age or Need? Public Policies for Older People*. Beverly Hills, California: Sage Publications.

Newman, W. M.
1973 *American Pluralism: A Study of Minority Groups and Social Theory*. New York: Harper and Row.

Ortega, S. T., R. D. Crutchfeld, and W. A. Rushing
1983 "Race Differences in Elderly Personal Well-Being." *Research on Aging* 5:101–18.

Osako, M. M.
1979 "Aging and Family among Japanese Americans: The Role of Ethnic Tradition in the Adjustment to Old Age." *The Gerontologist* 19:448–55.

Palmore, E.
1969 "Sociological Aspects of Aging." Pp. 47–61 in E. Busse and E. Pfeiffer (eds.), *Behavior and Adaptation in Late Life* (1st ed.). Boston: Little, Brown and Co.

1975   *The Honorable Elders: A Cross Cultural Analysis of Aging in Japan.*
        Durham, North Carolina: Duke University Press.
Palmore, E. B., and K. Manton
1973   "Ageism Compared to Racism and Sexism." *Journal of Gerontology*
        28:363–69.
Pitt, B.
1982   *Psycho-geriatrics: An Introduction to the Psychiatry of Old Age* (2nd
        ed.). Edinburgh, Scotland: Church Livingstone.
Porter, J.
1965   *The Vertical Mosaic.* Toronto: University of Toronto Press.
1979   *The Measure of Canadian Society: Education on Equality and Oppor-
        tunity.* Toronto: Gage Publishing.
Price, J.
1979   *Indians of Canada: Cultural Dynamics.* Scarborough, Ontario: Pren-
        tice-Hall.
Redfield, R.
1947   "The Folk Society." *American Journal of Sociology* 52:292–308.
Reisman, D.
1950   *The Lonely Crowd.* New York: Harper and Row.
Reitz, J. G.
1982   "Ethnic Group Control of Jobs." Research paper No. 133. Toronto:
        Centre for Urban and Community Studies, University of Toronto.
Rhoads, E. D.
1984   "Reevaluation of the Aging and Modernization Theory: The Samoan
        Evidence." *The Gerontologist* 24:242–50.
Richmond, A. H.
1972   *Ethnic Residential Segregation in Metropolitan Toronto.* Toronto:
        Toronto Survey Research Centre, York University.
Riley, M. W.
1971   "Social Gerontology and the Age Stratification of Society." *The Geron-
        tologist* 11:79–87.
1976   "Age Strata in Social Systems." Pp. 189–217 in R. Binstock, E. Shanas
        (eds.), *Handbook of Aging and the Social Sciences.* New York: Van
        Nostrand Reinhold.
Riley, M. W., M. Johnson, and A. Foner
1972   "The Succession of Cohorts." Pp. 515–82 in M. W. Riley, M. Johnson
        and A. Foner (eds.), *Aging and Society,* Vol. 3, *A Sociology of Age
        Stratification.* New York: Russell Sage Foundation.
Rioux, M.
1971   *Quebec in Question.* Toronto: James Lewis and Samuel.
Rioux, M., and Y. Martin
1964   *French-Canadian Society,* Vol. I. Toronto: McClelland and Stewart.
Roadburg, A.
1985   *Aging: Retirement, Leisure and Work in Canada.* Toronto: Methuen.
Roos, N. P. and Shapiro, E.
1981   "The Manitoba Longitudinal Study on Aging: Preliminary Findings on
        Health Care Utilization by the Elderly." *Medical Care* 19:64-67.
Rose, A.
1981   "The Jewish Elderly: Behind the Myths." Pp. 143–68 in M. Weinfeld, W.

Shaffir, and I. Cotler (eds.), *The Canadian Jewish Mosaic*. Rexdale, Ontario: John Wiley.

Rose, A. M.
1968   "The Subculture of Aging: A Framework for Research in Social Gerontology." Pp. 29–34 in B. L. Neugarten (ed.), *Middle Age and Aging*. Chicago: University of Chicago Press.

Rosenmayr, L., and E. Kockeis
1963   "Propositions for a Sociological Theory of Aging and the Family." *International Social Science Journal* 15:410–26.

Rosenthal, C. J.
1983   "Aging, Ethnicity and the Family: Beyond the Modernization Thesis." *Canadian Ethnic Studies* 15:1–16.
1986   "The Differentiation of Multigenerational Households." *Canadian Journal on Aging* 5:27–42.

Royal Commission on Bilingualism and Biculturalism
1970   *The Cultural Contribution of the Other Ethnic Groups*, Book IV. Ottawa: Queen's Printer.

Ryder, N. B.
1955   "The Interpretation of Origin Statistics." *The Canadian Journal of Economics and Political Science* 21:466–79.

Satariano, W. A., S. Albert, and S. H. Belle
1982   "Race, Age and Cancer Incidence: A Test of Double Jeopardy." *Journal of Gerontology* 37:642–47.

Schafer, A.
1985   "Ethical Dilemmas in Providing Care to the Elderly." Paper presented at Office of Continuing Care, Department of Health, In-Service Day, Winnipeg, Manitoba.

Schreiber, M. M.
1972   "The Aged of the 70's Perspective." Pp. 2–25 in L. Wilson (ed.), *Training Institute for Directors of Senior Centres*. Report of the Canadian Council on Social Development and Age and Opportunity Centre Inc., Winnipeg.

Schulz, J.
1976   *The Economics of Aging*. Belmont, California: Wadsworth.

Shanas, E.
1979   "The Family as a Support System in Old Age." *The Gerontologist* 19:169–74.

Shanas, E., and G. L. Maddox
1976   "Aging, Health and the Organization of Health Resources." Pp. 592–618 in R. H. Binstock and E. Shanas (eds.), *Handbook of Aging and the Social Sciences*. New York: Van Nostrand Reinhold.

Shibutani, T., and K. M. Kwan
1965   *Ethnic Stratification: A Comparative Approach*. New York: Collier-MacMillan.

Siegel, J. S.
1981   "Demographic Background for International Gerontological Studies." *Journal of Gerontology* 36:93–102.

Stanley, F. G.
1963   *Louis Riel*. Toronto: Ryerson Press.

Starrett, R. A., C. H. Mindel, and R. Wright
 1983 "The Role of the Kinship and Quasi-formal Support Systems in Predict-
ing the Use of Formal Social Services." Paper presented at the meetings
of the Midwest Council on Aging.

Statistics Canada
 1981 *Census of Canada.* Unpublished data.
 1984 *The Elderly in Canada.* Ottawa: Minister of Supply and Services.

Sterne, R. S., J. E. Phillips, and A. Rabushka
 1974 *The Urban Elderly Poor: Racial and Bureaucratic Conflict.* Lexington,
Massachusetts: D. C. Heath.

Stone, L. O., and S. Fletcher
 1985 "The Hypothesis of Age Patterns in Living Arrangement Passages." Unpublished paper, Statistics Canada, Ottawa.

Strain, L. A., and N. L. Chappell
 1984 "Social Support among Elderly Canadian Natives: A Comparison with
Elderly Non-Natives." Paper presented at the annual meetings of the
Canadian Association on Gerontology, Vancouver, British Columbia.

Strong, C.
 1984 "Stress and Caring for Elderly Relatives: Interpretations and Coping
Strategies in an American Indian and White Sample." *The Gerontologist* 24:251–56.

Sugiman, P., and H. K. Nishio
 1983 "Socialization and Cultural Duality among Aging Japanese Canadians."
Canadian Ethnic Studies 15:17–35.

Tepperman, L.
 1975 *Social Mobility in Canada.* Toronto: McGraw-Hill Ryerson.

Thomas, K., and A. Wister
 1984 "Living Arrangements of Older Women: The Ethnic Dimensions." *Journal of Marriage and the Family* 46:301–11.

Tilquin, C., C. Sicotte, T. Paquin, F. Tousignant, G. Gagnon, and P. Lambert
 1980 "The Physical, Emotional and Social Condition of an Aged Population
in Quebec." Pp. 222–31 in V. W. Marshall (ed.), *Aging in Canada:
Social Perspectives.* Don Mills, Ontario: Fitzhenry & Whiteside.

Ujimoto, K. V.
 1983 "Introduction: Ethnicity and Aging in Canada." *Canadian Ethnic
Studies* 15:i–vii.
 1986 "The Ethnic Dimension of Aging in Canada." In V. W. Marshall (ed.),
Aging in Canada. Don Mills, Ontario: Fitzhenry & Whiteside, forth-
coming.

Vallee, F. G.
 1981 "The Sociology of John Porter: Ethnicity as Anachronism." *Canadian
Review of Sociology and Anthropology* 18:636–50.

Vanderburgh, R. M.
 1982 "When Legend Falls Silent Our Ways are Lost: Some Dimensions of the
Study of Aging among Native Canadians." *Culture* 11:21–28.

Wanner, R. A., and P. L. McDonald
 1984 "The Vertical Mosaic in Later Life: Ethnicity and Retirement in
Canada." Paper presented at the annual meeting of the Canadian Association on Gerontology, Vancouver, B.C., November.

Watson, W. H.
1983   "Selected Demographic and Social Aspects of Older Blacks: An Analysis with Policy Implications." Pp. 42–49 in R. L. McNeely and J. L. Colen (eds.), *Aging in Minority Groups*. Beverly Hills, California: Sage Publications.

Weinfeld, M., W. Shaffir, and I. Cotler (eds.)
1981   *The Canadian Jewish Mosaic*. Rexdale, Ontario: John Wiley.

Wesley-King, S.
1983   "Service Utilization and the Minority Elderly: A Review." Pp. 241–49 in R. L. McNeely and J. L. Colen (eds.), *Aging in Minority Groups*. Beverly Hills, California: Sage Publications.

Wirth, L.
1945   "The Problem of Minority Groups." Pp. 347–72 in R. Linton (ed.), *The Science of Man in the World Crisis*. New York: Columbia University Press.

Wolf, J. H., N. Breslau, A. B. Ford, H. D. Ziegler, and A. Ward
1983   "Distance and Contacts: Interactions of Black Urban Elderly Adults with Family and Friends." *Journal of Gerontology* 38:465–71.

Wolinsky, F. D.
1983   "Health Care Policy and the Elderly: Short Term Cures and Long Term Catastrophies." Paper presented at the annual meeting of the Society for the Study of Social Problems, Detroit, Michigan.

Wong, P. T. P., and G. T. Reker
1985   "Stress, Coping and Well-Being in Anglo and Chinese Elderly." *Canadian Journal on Aging* 4:29–37.

Wu, F. Y. T.
1975   "Mandarin-Speaking Aged Chinese in the Los Angeles Area." *The Gerontologist* 15:271–75.

Young, T. K.
1984   "Indian Health Services in Canada: A Sociohistorical Perspective." *Social Science and Medicine* 18:257–64.

Zich, A.
1986   "Japanese Americans: Home at Last." *National Geographic* 169:512–39

INDEX

A

Aboriginal elderly, traditional, 48–53
    attitudes and activity of in
        Winnipeg, 1984, 52–53, t52
    ethnic identity retained, 50–51
    extended family support, 74–75
    low percentage of, 50
    Manitoba study, 51–52
    non-modernized, 50
    percentage of in population, 4, 8
    social policy for, designing, 96–97
    in U.S., 50, 51
Activity theory of aging, 14
African elderly, government program
    participation, 78–79
Age-as-leveller theory, 15, 18
Aged — See Elderly
Age stratification theory, 15–19
    age-as-leveller hypothesis, 18
    elderly as minority group, debate
        on, 15–18
    jeopardy hypotheses, 18
Aging
    activity theory of, 14
    defined, 3–4
    disengagement theory of, 14–15
    and ethnicity, perspectives on, 4–5
    as exchange, theory, 15
    modernization theory, 5, 19–27
    theories of, 14–26
Alzheimer's disease, 81
American blacks, extended family, 65
American eth-elders
    black vs. white support systems, 67
    European women, 67
    filial support, 68
    Japanese, 67
    Latino, 67–68
    race-ethnicity factor, 67

socioeconomic status and health,
    effect on kin support, 68
support vs. conflict, 68
and support patterns, 67–69
Anglo-conformity model in Canada,
    27–28
Anglos, 66
    in Canada, 66
Asian American informal networks,
    66
Asian elderly
    attitude to doctors, 88–89
    government program participation,
        78–79
Assimilation, 5
    civic change, 30
    cultural, 30
    and home language use, 40–42
    identificational change, 30
    marital, 30
    myth of British majority type,
        58–60
    vs. pluralism, 28–29
    receptional, 30
    structural, 30
Assimilation theory, 27–32
    compared to modernization theory,
        32–33, f33
    conflict theory, 31–32
    modified perspective, Gordon, 30
    multicultural pluralism,
        modifications of, 30–31
    primordial identity, 28
    seven dimensions of change,
        Gordon, 30

B

Baycrest Geriatric Centre, 54, 96
Bill 101, 32

Bimodal tendency, 36
Black elderly, health problems, 82
Black families and modernization, 26
British, 8
 gender differentials in immigration,
  11
 percentage of elderly in population,
  7
British charter type, designing social
  policy for, 100–101
British elderly
 Canadian-born, 10
 educational levels of, 35, t36
 foreign-born, 9
 heterogeneous group, 59
 largest charter group, 58
 living arrangements, 72
 marital status, 72
 in Newfoundland, 59
 number of children, 72, 73
 occupational status, 37, 39
 in Quebec, 59
 regional distribution, 46, 47
 religious affiliation, 42, 44, 45
 residence, 79, t80
 use of mother tongue, 40, 41

C

Canada
 Anglo-conformity model in early
  years, 27–28
 cultural and linguistic regions,
  1981, t49
 French-English power conflicts,
  31–32
 health care for elderly, 78
 multicultural pluralism, 29
 percentage of elderly in population,
  3–4, 7
Canada Health Survey, 18
Canadian eth-elders
 five ethnic groups, 70
 informal networks of, 69–75
  ethnic differentiation, 69–70
 non-identifiers, 71
Caucasian vs. Anglo, 66
Chicanos — See Mexican Americans

Chinese, 8
 gender differentials, immigration,
  11
Chinese elderly
 community-delivered services, 89
 educational levels of, 35, t36, 36
 living arrangements, 72
 low use of formal services, 76
 marital status, 72
 memories of discrimination, 1
 number of children, 72, 73
 occupational status, 37, 39
 religious affiliation, 46
 residence, 79, t80
 support needs, 69
 urban, 96
 use of mother tongue, 40, 41
Community
 defined, 92
 importance of, 92–94
 pool of resource persons, 93
 transportation problem, 93
Conflict theory, 31–32
 Marxian dialectic, 31
Counter-modernity, 25

D

Dementia in elderly, 81
Depression and elderly, 81
Disengagement theory of aging,
  14–15
 criticisms of, 14–15
Dutch elderly
 living arrangements, 72
 marital status, 72
 number of children, 72, 73
 occupational status, 37, 39
 religious affiliation, 42, 44, 45
 residence, 79, t80
 rural segregation, 37
 use of mother tongue, 41

E

East European women, 67
 family centredness, 91–92

Economic technology, 21
  as modernization, 37–40
Education
  as form of modernization, 35, 36–37
  modernization theory, 22–23
Elderly
  Canadian-born, 10, 11
  demographic variations in, 7–8
  foreign-born, 9–11
  gender differentials, 11
  lack of ethnic data on, 4
  as minority group
    arguments for and against, 17
    characteristics, 16
    debate on, 15–18
    theory, 15
  population growth in less-
    developed countries, 3
  as subculture, 15
  three groups of, 3
  tradition and history, as link to,
    1–2
Endogamy among Hutterites, 55
Eth-elders
  age vs. need, 87–88
  American, support patterns, 67–69
  Canadian, informal networks of,
    69–75
  dearth of Canadian studies on,
    66–67
  distribution by province, 1981, t47
  educational levels, 35–36, t36
  expressive/instrumental knowledge,
    27
  informal networks, 65–66
  intimate confidant needs, factors
    affecting, 66
  meeting needs of, 88–92
  modernization's static view of, 26
  needs and social policy, 87–94
  occupational status of in 1981, t39
  percentage of in ten metropolitan
    centres of Canada, 1981, t38
  regional variations in, 46–48
  religion as support for, 42, 46
  religious affiliation, t44–45
  shift to English language use, 1971,
    t43
  and social change, 35–46
  status needs not known, 65
  status problems, 5–6
  support for, 65–69
  types of, 46–60
    for policy purposes, 94–101
    by socioeconomic status and
      degree of urbanization, f95
    on traditional-modern
      continuum, f61
  use of formal services, 75–78
    in Canada, 78–80
Ethnic group membership,
  supportiveness of, 73–74
Ethnicity
  and aging, failure to study, 13
  assimilation theory, 5, 27–32
  cumulative disadvantages affecting
    need for care, 80–83
  defined, 2
  effect on living arrangements, 64
  foci of identification, 2–3
  as impediment to upward mobility,
    28
  informal networks, 65–66
  lack of data on elderly, 4
  living arrangements by, 1981, t71
  by marital status aged 65 years and
    over, 1981, t70
  and modernization theory, 26–27
  number of children born by, 1981,
    t73
  and perceived quality of life, 19
  by type of residence, Manitoba,
    1977, t80
Ethnic minorities, 3
Ethnos, 32
European prairie farm elders, 55–56
Evaluation research, 105–106
  outcome (summative), 105
  process (formative), 105
Exchange theory, 5, 23–24
  four balancing operations, 24
  static view of elderly, 26–27
Exogamy, 30
Extended family
  modified, 74
  as support network, 73–74

F

Families
 ethnicity vs. modernization, 26
 isolated nuclear, 74
FLQ movement, Quebec, 31
Folk society, 2
Formal services
 age-based, 87–88
 agency personnel, insensitivity,
  89–90
 allowing elderly to remain at
  home, 91
 community, importance of, 92–94
 delivered by ethnic group
  members, 89
 ethnic group control of, 90
 ethnic referral, 91
 family therapy, 91
 government programs,
  participation in, 78–79
 by income and education level, 77
 Indian preference for culturally
  relevant services, Winnipeg,
  1984, t90
 lack of Canadian data, 78
 lack of use by eth-elders, 75–78
 specific ethnic variations in use of,
  77–78
 supplemented by informal network,
  76–77
French, 8
 percentage of elderly in population,
  7
French Canadians
 language-assimilation fears, 40
 non-assimilation of, 29
French charter minority elderly,
  56–58
 modernization, 57
 regional differences, 56
 village of St. Denis, 57
French charter type, designing social
  policy for, 99–100
French elderly
 Canadian-born, 10
 educational levels of, 35–36, t36
 family support, 71
 foreign-born, 9
 living arrangements, 72
 marital status, 72
 number of children, 72, 73
 occupational status, 37, 39
 regional distribution, 46, 47
 religious affiliation, 42, 44, 45
 residence, 79, t80
 use of mother tongue, 40, 41
Friend, ethnic meaning variations, 75

G

Gender differentials in eth-elders, 11
German elderly
 occupational status, 37, 39
 religious affiliation, 42, 44, 45
 rural segregation, 37
 use of mother tongue, 41
Gerontology
 adjustment studies, 13
 social, 14
Government programs, eligibility by
  age or need, 87–88
Greek elderly
 religious affiliation, 42, 44, 45
 residence, 79, t80
 use of mother tongue, 41
Grey powers, 95

H

Health
 broad definition of, 101
 Canadian ethnic indicators, 82–83
 concerns of elderly, 81
 ethnic variations, in degree of, 82
 perceived, 81–82
 poverty, effect on, 82
 and reference group effect, 18–19
Health care
 in Canada, 78
 delivery, basic principles, 101–102
 ethnic variations in use, 79
Health technology, 20–21
Hispanic elderly, low use of formal
  services, 76

Hutterites, 29, 31, 65
  European prairie farm elders, 55

I

Immigration, gender differentials, 11
Indian caregivers of elderly natives,
  89
Indians, aged aboriginal, 1
Indians, reserve, live-in grandparents,
  70
Informal network
  Canadian elderly, 74
  ethnicity as factor in, 75
  as supplement to formal services,
  76–77
Intimacy-at-a-distance, 74
Inuit, 48. See also Native peoples
  elderly, 50
  regional distribution of, 48
Isolated nuclear family, 74
Italian elderly, 8
  educational levels of, 35, t36
  language conflict, Quebec, 32
  living arrangements, 72
  number of children, 72, 73
  occupational status, 37, 39, 40
  religious affiliation, 42, 44, 45
  residence, 79, t80
  use of formal services, 77
  use of mother tongue, 41

J

Japanese Americans, 64
  assistance for, 67
  health of, 82
Japanese elderly
  language as barrier to services,
  88–89
  memories of WWII imprisonment,
  1
Jeopardy theories, 15, 18, 81
Jewish elderly
  educational levels of, 35, t36
  memories of holocaust, 1

non-urban, 96
  occupational status, 37, 39, 40
  percentage of elderly in group's
  population, 4, 7–8
  religious affiliation, 42, 44, 45
  urban, 53–55
  diversity among, 53–54
  high status types, 94–96
  myths about, 54
  non-assimilated, 53
  providing for needs of, 54–55
  use of mother tongue, 41

L

Labelling theory, 15
Language
  as factors in meeting eth-elders'
  needs, 88–89
  as measure of ethnic identity, 40
  shift toward use of English, 41, t43
  use of mother tongue among
  elderly, 40–41
Latin Americans, government
  program participation, 78–79
Long-term institutional care, by
  ethnicity, 79, t80
Lord Durham, 27

M

Marital status, gender differentials, 11
Mennonites, 28
Mexican Americans
  informal networks, 66
  low use of formal services, 76
  modernization vs. ethnicity, 26
Middle old, the, 3
Minority, defined, 16
Modernization
  Berger's definition, 25
  economic technology as, 37–40
  education as, 35–36
  and ethnicity, 26–27
  exchange theory, 23–24
  health technology, 20–21

influence on religious affiliation, 46
processes, 19
  flow chart, 20
system overload, 26
urbanism as, 36–37
value system, effect on, 64
Modernization theory, 5, 19–27
  compared to assimilation theory,
    32–33, f33
  criticisms of, 23–25
  economic technology, 21
  education, 22–23
  exceptions to, 23
  modifications, 25–26
  urbanization, 21–22
Mortality, lowered, 20
Multicultural pluralism, 28–29
  modification of theory, 30–31

N

Native people — See also Aboriginal
    elderly, traditional
  health of, 82–83
  informal networks, 69–70
  rural segregation, 37
Needs assessments, 106
Newfoundland, low urbanization, 59
New fundamentalism, Muslims, 25
Non-identifiers, 100

O

Occupational status
  modern technology, 37–40
  regional link, 40
Old old, the, 3

P

Parti, Québécois, 31
Pension plans, ethnicity as factor in
    receipt of, 79
Polish elderly, 8
  educational level of, 35, t36
  occupational status, 39, 40

percentage of in population, 7
religious affiliation, 42, 44, 45
use of formal services, 76, 77
Portuguese elderly
  educational levels of, 35, t36
  foreign-born, 10
  religious affiliation, 42, 44, 45
  residence, 79, t80
  use of mother tongue, 42
Power conflict, 31
Primary-group relations, effect on
    status and ethnicity, 63–64
Primordial identity, 28

Q

Quebec, modernization of, 57–58
Quiet Revolution, 31, 57

R

Reference-group effect, 18–19
Religion
  Roman Catholics, 42
  as support for eth-elders, 42, 44–46
Research requirements for social
    policy, 102–105
  cohort vs. age differences, 104–105
  comparative data, 103
  cross-sequential designs, 105
  longitudinal and cross-sectional
    data, 104
  multiplicity of factors, 103–104
  several studies of same
    phenomenon, 103
Residence, ethnic variations in, 79
Residential segregation, 22
Retirement age, institutionalization
    of, 20–21
Rural high status type, 97–98
Rural low status type, 96–97
Rural prairie eth-elders
  designing social policy for, 97–98
Rural segregation, reduced service
    availability, 93
Russians, foreign-born elderly, 10

S

St. Denis, 57, 99
St. Pascal, 58, 100
Scandinavians
  occupational status, 37, 39
  religious affiliation, 42, 44, 45
  rural segregation, 37
  use of mother tongue, 41
Social gerontology, 14
Social policy
  age vs. need, 87–88
  British charter types, 100–101
  eth-elder types, 94–101
  evaluation research and needs
    assessments, 105–106
  French charter type, 99–100
  research requirements, 102–105
  rural high status type, 97–98
  rural low status type, 96–97
  urban high status type, 94–96
  urban low status type, 98–99
  visible minorities, 99
Social roles and age strata, 15
Social segregation, 22
Spanish elderly, support system, 67
Status
  assimilation theory, 6
  eight concepts of, 25
  modernization theory, 5–6
  retirement, effect on, 21
  social, evaluating by cultural and
    ethnic factors, 64
  urbanization, effect on, 21–22
Support patterns, American eth-
    elders, 67–69
System overload, 26

T

Third world elderly, 79
Tradition-directed person, 2

U

Ukrainian elderly, 1–2, 8
  educational levels of, 35, t36
  family support, 70
  occupational status, 37, 39
  percentage of in population, 7
  religious affiliation, 42, 44, 45
  rural segregation, 37
Urban high status type, 94–96
Urbanism as modernization, 36–37
Urbanization, 21–22
  geographic mobility, 21–22
  social mobility, 22
Urban low status type, 98–99

V

Value system, impact on
    modernization process, 64
Vertical Mosaic, The, 28
Visible minorities, designing social
    policy for, 99

Y

Young old, the, 3